Christian Cognitive Behavioral Therapy

Samaria M Colbert

© 2018 All Rights Reserved Samaria M. Colbert

The Book: Christian Cognitive Behavioral Therapy

Scripture quotations are from the Holy Bible. The New King James Version: Containing the Old and New Testaments. Nashville TN: Thomas Nelson, 1985. The Message Bible: Eugene H. Peterson, 2002. New American Standard Bible

Preface

We are living in a different world. Natural disaster, calamities, wars, and rumors of war. At the time of me writing this book, there have been 18 school shootings this year. People need Jesus like never before. These world events have an impact on mental health. Those who are Christian are not immune. According to Christianity Today in 2015 they reported that 1,500 pastors leave the ministry every month. According to the Schaeffer Institute, 70 percent of pastors constantly fight depression, and 71 percent experience burn out. We are now seeing an alarming trend where pastors and church leaders commit suicide.

My point is not to give you a doom and gloom outlook. We can no longer ignore the need for Christian counseling. We also can't ignore mental health. Many people don't know that basic Christian counseling is not an effective way to address mental health alone. Many who are certified Christian counselors have no idea how to address mental illness from a Christian perspective. Mental health counseling has its own field of study and specialty that is often overlooked in Christian counseling alone. To my dismay, many mental health therapists have never been taught the integrative approach to address an individual's mental health through faith while incorporating their relationship with Christ and the Holy Spirit as the most effective way to address mental illness.

When I went through my initial training years ago, as a mental health specialist I learned nothing about incorporating an individual's spiritual life through Christ.

On a personal note, I am a dedicated Christian. I have been in the mental health field for 13 years now. As I have offered mental health treatment I realized that secular mental health treatment only addresses symptoms, an individual may never get to full healing and wholeness. Christ came to heal and set us free from all emotional wounds. Imagine the dichotomy (the contrast between two worlds).

As I have grown in my personal relationship with Christ. I have grown as a mental health clinician. The Lord began to spark hope in me. He allowed me to spend hours, years, studying and preparing to do mental health counseling His way. One of the most life transformational insights that the Father gave me was that in Him alone freedom is found. That doesn't mean we do away with the mental health strategies. So as the Lord began to guide me, He showed me how all counseling, including mental health counseling, originated from scripture. What the secular world has done is taken out the name of Jesus, the works of the cross, its teaching, counseling techniques out and then called it by a different name. They don't want to believe in Jesus so they promote healing absent from Him. Therefore most mental health therapy is helpful but not healing or life transforming. It helps you maintain, to cope but it **NEVER** delivers you or sets you free. Therefore the average patient sees a therapist their entire life. While an individual who seeks Christian mental health, counseling may see a therapist six months or less.

When God gave me this divine revelation it changed my life. I realized that everything I learned in graduate school and in my life's work as a therapist originated from the bible. When I do counseling I simply put the cross and Jesus back into its rightful place and give credit back to its original owner. This is true and real effective Christian mental health counseling. This work has transformed my life as a therapist and as an overcomer. I too suffered from depression, anxiety, and suicidal thoughts, but I write to you today healed, set free by the blood of Jesus.

God has also allowed me to establish my own private practice Kingdom Creative Counseling, where we offer mental health counseling and treatment from heaven's perspective.

In the book; Christian Cognitive Behavioral Therapy I will teach you how to implement one of the most effective therapeutic strategies known today but we will put the emphasis back on its original owner. We will learn to implement cognitive behavioral therapy through Christ, hence the term Christian Cognitive Behavioral Therapy.

Be on the lookout for training seminars, and other resource materials that will help you minister effective mental health treatment through the cross of Jesus Christ.

Let our journey begin.

The first in this series is this book that will break down the principles of Christian based mental health treatment. **This book is meant to assist LICENSED mental health counselors, psychologist, Christian counselors and Christian leaders who ALREADY HAVE A BACKGROUND, FORMAL TRAINING, OR LICENSURE IN THE COUNSELING FIELD.**

A coach or consultant should not treat psychological or mental health issues that should be addressed by a trained counselor. No, you are not going to be able to take one class or get a six-week certificate and be fully trained to treat deep-seated psychological issues whether you are Christian or not. That is why we therapist/clinicians/counselors get master's degrees and doctorates in the counseling field. Don't think you can cheat the process. Counseling is a ministry that takes YEARS to prepare for like any other ministry.

Yes, I did just put all that in bold. These series of teachings are meant to be an addition to the back ground in mental health counseling you already have, a stepping stone, NOT a onetime only training. You will not be able to finish this book and then be able to say you are a counselor who does this work.

Samaria Colbert is a licensed therapist. She does strictly adhere HIPPA laws that govern confidentiality and Tarasoff laws; with the exceptions of intent to harm of oneself or another. With that being said, in this book, the author does not release anything confidential or disclose of any identifying information about any of the clients she has treated past, present, or future.

Table of Contents

Chapter 1

What Is Christian Cognitive Behavioral Therapy?

Proverbs 23:7 (KJV)

7 For as he thinketh in his heart, so is he:

Cognitive means mental processes of perception, memory, judgment, and reasoning, as contrasted with emotional and willful processes. In layman's term cognitive refers to how you think. Cognition means the act or process of knowing, and perceiving. Basically, cognition refers to how you come to know and believe what you believe. Think about it no one comes to the earth believing a certain thing about themselves or the world. We are taught what to believe, how to think about ourselves and the world. Behavior refers to how you act. Therapy refers to the systematic act of treating mental and emotional wounds through the art of counseling.

The basic principle of cognitive behavior therapy is that thoughts, impact beliefs which then impact behavior. If we want to change how an individual behaves we must first change their thoughts.

A philosopher once said it is not what happens to you that matters but what you think about what happens to you that matters. For example, let's say your best friend betrayed you. You could think, "I will never trust again." Consequently, you go through life being defined but what someone did to you. Your narrative will be that every time you meet someone you will have difficulty trusting if you trust at all. However, if you say, "that was an opportunity for growth." Then your narrative becomes different. You are not defined by one moment in time or one person.

There was a story of two twin brothers who grew up with a father who was addicted to alcohol. One brother never drank alcohol in his life the other brother became addicted to alcohol. When one brother was asked, why he never became addicted to alcohol? He responded, "I watched my dad drink my entire life." When the other brother was asked how he became addicted to alcohol? He said, "I watched my dad drink my entire life." Your narrative (story, experience) is formed by how you perceive your experience.

There was the story of two salesmen. They were sent to go to a foreign country to see what the market was like to establish a shoe store in developing nations. One shoe salesmen got to the country and became very discouraged. He went back to his supervisors and said, "we can't build here no one wears shoes." The other salesmen went to the developing country at a different time. He came back excited, he told his superiors, "we need to start building right away, we are going to make tons of money, no one wears shoes here."

You see one saw the absence of shoes and a deficit, the other saw the absence of shoes as an opportunity to introduce a new product to a nation of people.

Think about it thirty years ago, no one thought they needed an i-phone, a computer or a tablet. Now we don't think of cell phones as luxury items but necessities. Most people including me won't go anywhere without their cell phone. Your thoughts impact what you believe, which then impacts how you act.

The Cognitive Triangle

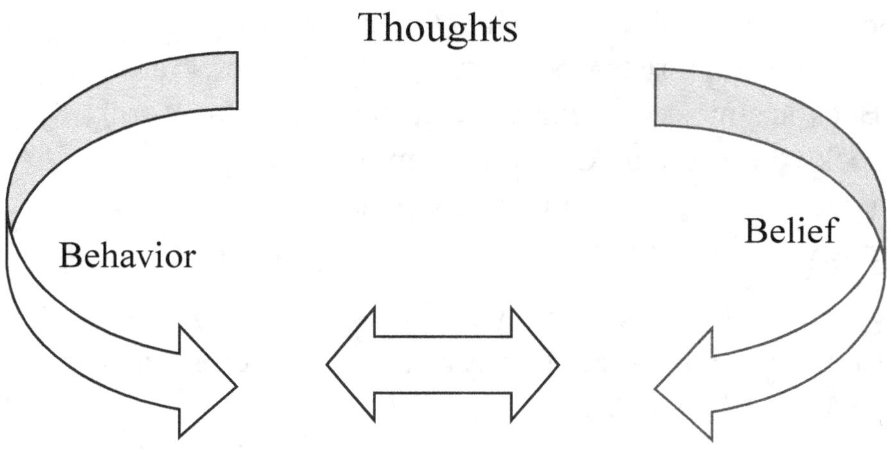

Where it all began:

We will first start with where CBT began in our history, however as stated in the preface CBT has been around since the beginning of time. The true beginnings are found in the Bible, going back to Genesis. We will also learn how CBT is similar and different from Christian cognitive behavioral therapy.

The beginnings of our history started with John B Watson and Rosalie Rayner who studied conditioning in the 1920's. Conditioning means the process of training. The theorist did a series of experiments called classical conditioning. They concluded that fear and other emotions could be conditioned (or trained) into us. Other behaviorist contributed to the field of include Mary Cover Jones who taught about unlearning fears in children. There are many others who contributed to the field of psychology because this is not a history book I won't bore you with the details. Other contributors included behaviorist Albert Alder, B.F. Skinner. Aaron T. Beck is a most well-known contributor. It was Aaron T Beck who is credited to have combined both behavior and cognition into what we now know as cognitive behavioral therapy.

Cognitive behavioral therapy is considered one of the most effective therapeutic interventions to address most mental health disorders.

Basic Principles of CBT:

According to Mcleod, CBT is based on the idea that how we think (cognition), how we feel (emotion) and how we act (behavior) all interact together. Specifically, our thoughts determine our feelings and our behavior.

Therefore, negative and unrealistic thoughts can cause us distress and result in problems. When a person suffers from psychological distress, the way in which they interpret situations becomes skewed, which in turn has a negative impact on the actions they take.

CBT aims to help people become aware of when they make negative interpretations, and of behavioral patterns which reinforce the distorted thinking. Cognitive therapy helps people to develop alternative ways of thinking and behaving which aim to reduce their psychological distress.

Mcleod. Saul (2015). Cognitive Behavioral Therapy. Retrieved from https://www.simplypsychology.org/cognitive-therapy.html. Retrieved on April 1, 2018

CBT Assumptions: (Saul McLeod)

• The cognitive approach believes that abnormality stems from faulty cognitions about others, our world and us. This faulty thinking maybe through cognitive deficiencies (lack of planning) or cognitive distortions (processing information inaccurately).

• These cognitions cause distortions in the way we see things; Ellis suggested it is through irrational thinking, while Beck proposed the cognitive triad.

• We interact with the world through our mental representation of it. If our mental representations are inaccurate or our ways of reasoning are inadequate then our emotions and behavior may become disordered.

Mcleod. S (2015). Cognitive Behavioral Therapy. Retrieved from https://www.simplypsychology.org/cognitive-therapy.html. Retrieved on April 2, 2018

There is much more to know about the foundations of CBT however now we must explore how cognitive behavioral therapy is really first and foremost founded in Christ, hence the term that I will use for the remainder of our study together Christian cognitive behavioral therapy. By the way, basic CBT in all its success is still very limited, one major missing component is that CBT has never addressed or attempted to address an individual's spiritual life. No matter how the research brags about how effective it is, it is not as successful as you think. I worked in community mental health for many years where we were trained habitually in CBT, we actually saw very few successes. I believe because it never introduces Christ or the Holy Spirit into the treatment modality. The behaviorist also never claimed to be Christian or believed in Christ. In fact, many don't believe in Jesus.

You can't teach what you don't know. This is why CBT helps some but never heals most. In Christ we want healing and wholeness to take place.

Before we begin we must understand how Christ really is the center of the therapeutic process. I did a radio interview a few months ago and I was asked how does counseling and therapy fit into the ministry?

My response was that counseling is the ministry of Christ, it is one of the primary reasons why He came.

Isaiah tells us the mission of Christ.

Isaiah 61:1-3 (KJV)

61 The Spirit of the Lord God is upon me; because the Lord hath anointed me to preach good tidings unto the meek; he hath sent me to bind up the brokenhearted, to proclaim liberty to the captives, and the opening of the prison to them that are bound;

2 To proclaim the acceptable year of the Lord, and the day of vengeance of our God; to comfort all that mourn;

3 To appoint unto them that mourn in Zion, to give unto them beauty for ashes, the oil of joy for mourning, the garment of praise for the spirit of heaviness; that they might be called trees of righteousness, the planting of the Lord, that he might be glorified.

When the scripture talks about brokenhearted he was not referring to a heart condition, although Jesus heals cardiac problems. Brokenhearted means, overwhelmed by grief, depression or disappointment. He came for the captives. Notice the scripture uses the words captives and prisoners. The scriptures tell us that a captive wasn't just someone who served time in prison. A captive is a person that is in mental, emotional, physical bondage. Other significant words that are significant for the counseling profession includes mourning, heaviness, vengeance. Mourning means deep sadness. A spirit of heaviness is something that weighs you down emotionally. Heaviness is anxiety, sorrow, grief, dread, anxious care.

My point is this is the primary reasons why Jesus came. Jesus came as the savior, but He also brought with Him the ministry of the counselor. The scripture is full of counselors and teachers. The Bible encourages us to seek counseling.

Proverbs 11:14 (KJV)

14 Where no counsel is, the people fall: but in the multitude of counselors there is safety.

There is a safe place found when we seek counseling. Still, the scripture also put criteria on how and who we should seek counseling from.

Psalm 1:1 (KJV)

1 Blessed is the man that walketh not in the counsel of the ungodly, nor standeth in the way of sinners, nor sitteth in the seat of the scornful.

Scripture doesn't tell us not to seek counseling, it says don't seek ungodly counseling, don't seek counseling from sinners or the scornful. A scornful person is someone who openly and unapologetically speaks ill, dislikes others.

I believe this is why many Christians don't want to seek counseling, the secular world has hijacked what belonged to God and the assumption is that when you seek counseling you are going outside of the realm of God to do so. This is a myth. When you seek counseling make sure the therapist is a Christian, in word and in integrity. Meaning if they claim to be a Christian but openly living sinful lives we are not to seek counseling from them. We as Christian therapist must make sure our private lives line up to the word of God so that we can be fit to be used for the master's use.

I know of many therapists who don't know God. They would be glad to sit and counsel you. Therapist are taught to not push their personal views about religion or politics onto the client's that they treat. In some ways that is not a bad thing, if I am seeking counseling I don't want to hear your political views about the president or how you feel about immigration. Yet, I have met with some counselors who are directly opposed to Christian and Christian values but will sit and listen to you about your faith as long as your insurance pays. I believe it is perfectly fine for a client to ask the therapist about their Christian values. If they decline to answer, then look for another counselor. Be respectful about it. We counselors may not want to tell you very deeply personal things about us. Asking the counselor his or her age, her marital status, weight, whether they have children etc is up to their discretion to respond to. Respect their boundaries. When I was in my twenties I had clients discriminate against me for being in my twenties, or for not having children. So, in the past, I would decline to answer deeply personal questions. That was many years ago I am more comfortable now but that is still at my discretion. My point is a true Christian counselor should be unafraid of telling you about their faith stance, once you ask.

Luke 9:26 (NKJV)

26 For whoever is ashamed of Me and My words, of him the Son of Man will be ashamed when He comes in His own glory, and in His Father's, and of the holy angels.

Because I am in private practice all my marketing material such as business cards, websites and brochures always make my biblical stance clear.

My point is we counselors must be clear that Christ is our first supervisor, we are stewards of the gift He has given us.

Because Christ ministry was that of a counselor, the standards, and strategies by which we counsel are first found in the bible. Cognitive behavioral therapy really originated from the bible. Just because some theorist or behaviorist takes credit for what God established, doesn't mean they are the true originators of it. Just like we're told that Christopher Columbus discovered America, we now know this to not be true. Nevertheless, even if Christopher Columbus really did discover America, it was God who created the entire world. Discover means to find something, to uncover what is hidden. But, to create means to bring into existence.

To truly understand the biblical originator of cognitive behavior therapy we must understand the original intent that God created it for. There is much more to say.

Chapter 2

Christian Cognitive Behavioral Therapy

Part II

Genesis 3:11 (NKJV)

11 And He said, "Who told you that you were naked? Have you eaten from the tree of which I commanded you that you should not eat?"

Where do thoughts come from? I know I have asked a silly question but go with me I am going somewhere. I will ask the same question in a different way. Where do thoughts originate from? Tsahi Rosenbluth, states in a 2013 article that thoughts come from outside of our bodies. He then went on to teach that there are three stages of thoughts,

From the moment of their inception and until the moment they become an action, however small, our thoughts pass through three stages. The first stage is an inborn trait - Potential. The individual born to be a motor mechanic will never entertain thoughts of being a fashion designer since this choice is not included in their inborn potentials.

The second stage is -Understanding. This is the stage where we analyze the thoughts we have received and attempt to adapt them to our own unique and individual world of concepts. For example, if I wake up and think that I need to find a new job, I'll immediately start looking for a job in familiar areas. If I work at a bar or coffee shop, I'll look for a new job in the service sector, in customer service but I won't look for work in another profession, such as a cosmetician since this requires knowledge that I don't have.

The third stage is- Realization. This stage acts on the original thought and directs me to ways of finding a new job: the internet, by asking at restaurants if they need new staff, what to wear and what to take with me, how to get there (by car or public transport), how to introduce myself etc. This stage also leads on to the actual implementation of the thought - looking for a job.

Rosenbluth, T (2013, October 15). Where do our thoughts originate? Retrieved from https://www.israelnationalnews.com/Blogs/Message.aspx/5343 on February 28, 2018

Interesting perspective. Yet again we must look at the original intent and creator of a thing. Therefore, we must look at the original creator. Only the creator of a thing knows the true purpose of why He created it. Thoughts originated from God. How do we know this? Because scripture tells us that God created all things.

All thing includes thoughts, even though they are invisible.

Colossians 1:16-17 (NKJV)

16 For by Him all things were created that are in heaven and that are on earth, visible and invisible, whether thrones or dominions or principalities or powers. All things were created through Him and for Him.

17 And He is before all things, and in Him all things consist.

We were created in the image and likeness of God, therefore from the beginning, we were created to think, behave and to conduct ourselves like God. I didn't say we were gods, I said we were created in the likeness of God. Every parent knows that the child reflects who they are even though there is a difference between the child and the parent.

Genesis 1:26 (NKJV)

26 Then God said, "Let Us make man in Our image, according to Our likeness; let them have dominion over the fish of the sea, over the birds of the air, and over the cattle, over all[a] the earth and over every creeping thing that creeps on the earth."

Genesis 1:27 (NKJV)

27 So God created man in His own image; in the image of God He created him; male and female He created them.

Life would be so simple if we all just talked and thought like God. There would be no need for cognitive behavioral therapy, no one would be depressed, anxious, or worried. Unfortunately, life is not so simple.

So, if we were created in the image and likeness to think like Him what happened? I am sure you know but let's discuss this further.

Man was introduced to another form of thinking that was not God. Let's go back to our original text; Genesis 3:11

Genesis 3:11 Living Bible (TLB)

11 "Who told you you were naked?" the Lord God asked. "Have you eaten fruit from the tree I warned you about?"

Told (tell) means communicate information, facts, or news to someone in spoken or written words. It is an unconscious action that is thought to betray an attempted deception. Notice the words betray and deception or in other words to deceive. Deceive means deceit, deceitfulness, duplicity, double-dealing, fraud, cheating, trickery, chicanery, deviousness, slyness, wiliness, guile, bluff, lying, pretense, treachery.

In the beginning, Adam and Eve only knew about God and God-thoughts what happened? From the beginning, God always gave the man the power of choice. Choice means the right to make decisions. He tells them what to do it is up to them to decide whether or not they want to obey.

Genesis 2: 16-17 (NKJV)

Genesis 2:16 New King James Version (NKJV)

16 And the Lord God commanded the man, saying, "Of every tree of the garden you may freely eat;

17 but of the tree of the knowledge of good and evil you shall not eat, for in the day that you eat of it you shall surely die."

Man decided to disobey God, but why? We have to go back to the "tell" or "told" word we used.

Genesis 3:1-7 Living Bible (TLB)

1 The serpent was the craftiest of all the creatures the Lord God had made. So the serpent came to the woman. "Really?" he asked. "None of the fruit in the garden? God says you mustn't eat any of it?"

2-3 "Of course we may eat it," the woman told him. "It's only the fruit from the tree at the center of the garden that we are not to eat. God says we mustn't eat it or even touch it, or we will die."

4 "That's a lie!" the serpent hissed. "You'll not die! 5 God knows very well that the instant you eat it you will become like him, for your eyes will be opened—you will be able to distinguish good from evil!"

6 The woman was convinced. How lovely and fresh looking it was! And it would make her so wise! So she ate some of the fruit and gave some to her husband, and he ate it too.

7 And as they ate it, suddenly they became aware of their nakedness, and were embarrassed. So they strung fig leaves together to cover themselves around the hips.

So, what happened is satan who is the deceiver implanted alternative ideas, and information through verbal communication. Although thoughts originated from God, the first deception happened when satan decided that he no longer wanted to be a servant of God. He first deceived himself. When Adam and Eve were created and satan set out to deceive them and unfortunately, he was successful at his plan. All satan had to do was introduce an alternative thought pattern that was contrary to what God had already spoken. They chose to believe what satan said more then what God said, and the fall of man happened in that instant.

Believe it or not this, in essence, is the foundation of Christian Cognitive Behavioral therapy. Within the basic cognitive behavioral therapy, the primary strategy is for the therapist and the client, to look at a pattern of thought, determine the evidence to support that thought and then replace that thought with a more realistic and true way of thinking. If we want to eliminate negative thoughts we must replace negative self-defeating thoughts with positive thoughts, hence CBT.

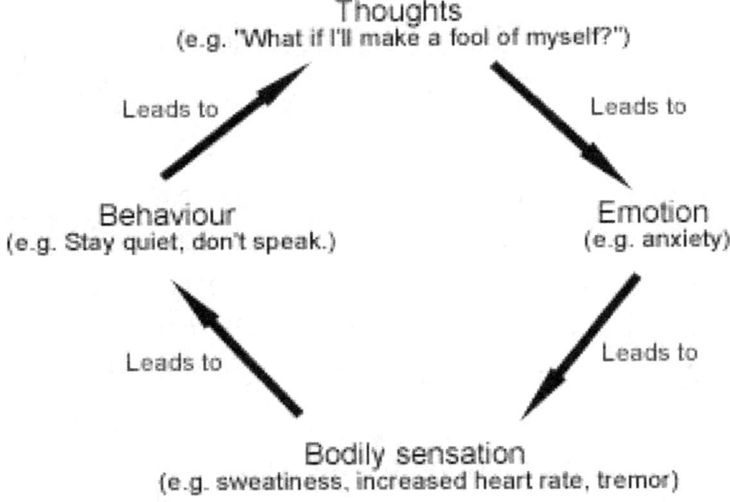

Remember we said thoughts originated from God. Yet we now live in a word where there are many different schools of thought and ways of learning that are alternative to the very will of God. God's thoughts are not our thoughts.

Isaiah 55:8-9 King James Version (KJV)

8 For my thoughts are not your thoughts, neither are your ways my ways, saith the Lord.

9 For as the heavens are higher than the earth, so are my ways higher than your ways, and my thoughts than your thoughts.

In Christian Cognitive Behavioral Therapy, we analyze our thoughts, we don't compare them to ourselves or our own truth, we then compare those thoughts to the word of God. The strategy is to remove our own negative self-defeating thoughts, replace them with the word of God and what God has to say about us.

Secular CBT looks like this:

Cognitive Therapy Thought Record				www.CognitiveTherapyGuide.org
Situation	Initial Thought	Negative Thinking	Evidence for this Thinking	Alternative Thinking
I made a mistake at work.	I feel like a failure. If people knew the real me, they wouldn't like me.	This is self-labeling and disqualifying the positives.	I'm hard on myself. I've had some successes. I don't always succeed, but I do sometimes. People have complimented me on my work. It's when I try to be perfect that I feel overwhelmed and disappointed in myself. I'm damaging my self-esteem. My negativity will affect my relationships and possibly my health. I'll become exhausted.	I don't have to succeed at everything. Making a mistake doesn't mean that I fail at everything. I want to get rid of this negative thinking. I'm going to celebrate my victories, and focus on the positives. The next time I make a mistake, I won't dwell on the negatives and waste my energy. Instead I'll focus on what I can learn from my mistake.
Describe the situations that led to your unpleasant feelings.	What thoughts first entered your mind?	Identify the negative thinking behind your initial thought.	Look at the evidence for and against this thinking. Have you been in a similar situation before? What strengths do you bring to this situation? Look at the whole picture.	Once you've considered the facts, write down a healthier way of thinking.

* This thought record template can be copied without restrictions for personal use.

Christian Cognitive Behavioral Therapy Looks Like This:

Situation	Initial thought	Negative thinking	What does the word of God have to say?	Alternative Thinking
"I made a mistake at work."	"I feel like a failure."	"This is self-labeling and disqualifying the positive."	Philippians 4:13 (KJV) 13 I can do all things through Christ which strengthened me. Romans 8:1 (KJV) 8 There is therefore now no condemnation to them which are in Christ Jesus, who walk not after the flesh, but after the Spirit.	"I made a mistake at work but I can still do all things because Christ lives in me." "I don't have to stay in guilt for a mistake because Christ Jesus lives in me."

Are you seeing the difference? The main reason why CCBT works is that it takes our thoughts off ourselves. CCBT works because it incorporates the supernatural power of the word of God. The more word we get in us the more powerful we will be.

Hebrews 4:12 (KJV)

12 For the word of God is quick, and powerful, and sharper than any two-edged sword, piercing even to the dividing asunder of soul and spirit, and of the joints and marrow, and is a discerner of the thoughts and intents of the heart.

The word of God is not just affirmations, positive thinking or nice sayings to get us to think better of ourselves. No! the word of God gets in us and begins to transform, we put away the negative cognitions and patterns. We then begin to go back to the original intent of the creator and that is to think in the likeness of God. I gave you a lot of information I hope you are getting this. Let us look at another example of secular CBT.

AUTOMATIC THOUGHT RECORD

... mood worsening, fill in the chart below by asking yourself, **"What am I thinking and feeling right now?"**

Automatic Thoughts (ATs)	Emotion/s	Adaptive Response	
• What thought/s or image/s went through your mind? • How much did you believe the thought at the time (0-100%)?	• What emotion/s did you feel at the time? • How intense was the emotion (0-100%)?	• Which thinking styles did you engage in? • Use questions below to respond to the automatic thoughts/s. • How much do you believe each response (0-100%)?	
"He is angry with me" (90%) (personalizing, mind reading, jumping to conclusions)	sad (55%) scared (90%)	1. Evidence that my thought is TRUE (30%) • He didn't call on time • He has been angry before NOT TRUE (70%) • He has forgotten to call before • We have been getting along well • He seemed to be in a good mood earlier • There's nothing he would be mad about 2. Would others agree that my thoughts is true? • Probably not (50%) 3. Alternative explanations (70%) • He innocently forgot to call • He got busy and couldn't call • He's on his way home now • He's on a business call now 4. If a friend has this thought, I would say: • Don't worry, nothing is wrong (40%) • You are overreacting (65%) • Wait until you really know (60%) • If he is angry, you can deal with it (95%) • You haven't done anything wrong (95%)	

Automatic Thought Record for Christian Cognitive Behavior Therapy

Automatic Thoughts (ATs)	Emotion/s	Adaptive Response
What thoughts went through your mind? What did you believe about the thought?	"What emotions did you feel at the time?"	"what thinking did you engage in and how can we confront that thought with the word of God to think differently?"
"he is angry at me" (personalizing, mind reading, jumping to conclusions)	Anger Frustrated Afraid	Proverbs 29:25 (KJV) 25 The fear of man bringeth a snare: but whoso putteth his trust in the Lord shall be safe." "Whether my thought is true or not if I trust in God it doesn't matter what a person has to say about me. I don't have to be afraid."

Hopefully, you are seeing the difference. The truth of the matter is sometimes you can cross every T and dot every I, and someone will have an issue with you even with your good intentions. You can't be bound by the opinions of others. Christian Cognitive Behavioral Therapy is a strategic and systematic way of mental health treatment that first seeks to put the heart, mind, and thoughts of man, back to the original intent creation. When this happens we think and believe the way God thinks and believes about us. Remember as stated deception happened when a man believed the voice of the enemy satan above the voice of God.

This is the basis for all mental health conditions it is a psychological attack on the mind that renders us to begin to believe, think and act based upon the deception of thoughts that are originated by satan himself. **I am not saying nor am I implying that mental health conditions are demons.** I am stating that there is a spiritual undercurrent to most mental health conditions. Look at how deceptive thoughts happen from the Christian Cognitive Behavioral triangle.

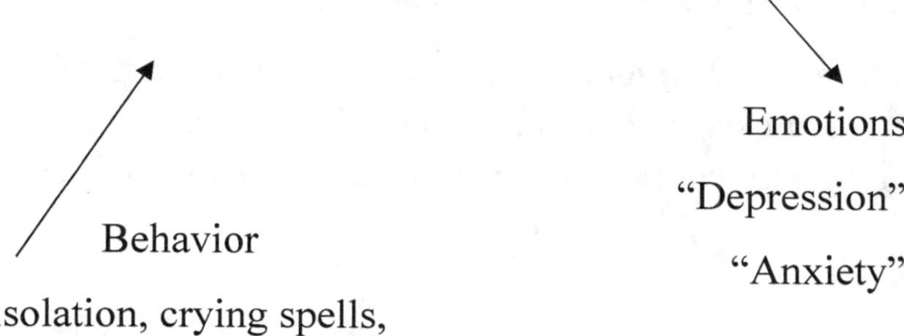

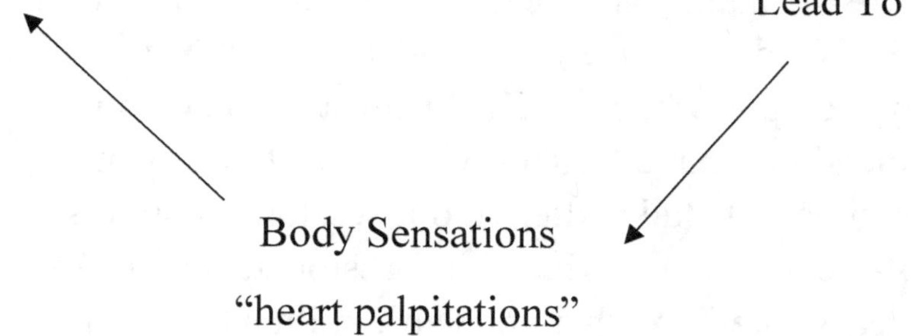

These thoughts create repetitive cycles. When we align our thoughts with the word of God, He breaks strongholds and cycles off of our lives.

Chapter 3

Guiding Principles of Christian Cognitive Behavioral Therapy

---

2 Corinthians 10:5 King James Version (KJV)

5 Casting down imaginations, and every high thing that exalteth itself against the knowledge of God, and bringing into captivity every thought to the obedience of Christ;

Before we discuss how to implement CCBT we must explore the main principles of CCBT as found in the word of God. They are the foundational truths that every therapist who uses CCBT must be clear and grounded in. I have a client who is a gifted carpenter and builder. He talks often in our sessions about his work because that is what he is passionate about. Any builder will tell you that you can't build a house or a structure if the foundation is not solid.

Matthew 7:24-27 King James Version (KJV)

24 Therefore whosoever heareth these sayings of mine, and doeth them, I will liken him unto a wise man, which built his house upon a rock:

25 And the rain descended, and the floods came, and the winds blew, and beat upon that house; and it fell not: for it was founded upon a rock.

26 And every one that heareth these sayings of mine, and doeth them not, shall be likened unto a foolish man, which built his house upon the sand:

27 And the rain descended, and the floods came, and the winds blew, and beat upon that house; and it fell: and great was the fall of it.

We cannot fully implement CCBT without understanding the foundation of the word of God. We know as counselors and therapist even after the work of counseling is done, that doesn't stop the storms of life from coming. Nevertheless, if the CCBT has been worked through correctly the client is still able to handle life storms because we taught them foundation. In most cases, they won't have to keep coming back to therapy every time the struggles of life come. The next few principles will establish the foundation for Christian Cognitive Behavioral Therapy. Let's identify the principles of God thoughts.

Principle 1: According to the word of God how we think dictates how we see ourselves.

Proverbs 23:7 (KJV)

7 For as he thinketh in his heart, so is he.

Principle 2:

According to scripture thinking doesn't happen in the head rather it happens in our heart.

Principle 3:

You can control your thoughts and dictate what your mind continues to play over and over again.

Principle 4:

In order to gain mastery over our thoughts, we have to intentionally align them with the word of God, and intentionally discard any thought that doesn't fall in line what God says.

Philippians 4:6-9 (KJV)

6 Be careful for nothing; but in every thing by prayer and supplication with thanksgiving let your requests be made known unto God.

7 And the peace of God, which passeth all understanding, shall keep your hearts and minds through Christ Jesus.

8 Finally, brethren, whatsoever things are true, whatsoever things are honest, whatsoever things are just, whatsoever things are pure, whatsoever things are lovely, whatsoever things are of good report; if there be any virtue, and if there be any praise, think on these things.

9 Those things, which ye have both learned, and received, and heard, and seen in me, do: and the God of peace shall be with you.

Principle 5: To align my thoughts, with the word of God I must know the word of God. In order to know the word of God, I must commit to study and reading the word of God.

Principle 6: For complete healing to come we must invoke the Holy Spirit to help to guard and guide our thoughts.

Principle 7: In Christian Cognitive Behavioral Therapy, there is a beginning, a middle and an end to therapy. Therefore, CCBT is time-limited, structured, client-centered, and Christ-focused.

Principle 8: Christian Cognitive Behavioral Therapy, teaches the client to identify their thoughts and feelings, to determine their faulty nature.

Principle 9: Christian Cognitive Behavioral Therapy also employs the scripture principles of grace and forgiveness. Grace means the unearned, and unmerited, (undeserved) favor, kindness and from God.

We understand that grace is not earned it is received as a gift. Still, we also understand that grace is not a license nor is it a reason to continue in sin. Grace is what we employ and welcome into our hearts and minds to not allow past failures, poor choices, and sins to allow us to live in condemnation and emotional turmoil.

Forgiveness is the intentional act of releasing, to stop holding anger or resentment towards(someone) for an offense, flaw, or mistake. Forgiveness is the conscious, deliberate decision to release feelings of resentment or vengeance toward a person or group who has harmed you, regardless of whether they deserve your forgiveness. Forgiveness does not mean forgetting, nor does it mean condoning or excusing offenses.

Forgiveness (n.d). Retrieved. Greater Good Magazine. https://greatergood.berkeley.edu/topic/forgiveness/definition. Retrieved March 1, 2018

We must employ grace and forgiveness in CCBC because often our thoughts, are guilt-ridden and shame-based. To be free from guilt and shame whether it be warranted or unwarranted we must understand how to implement the principles of God thoughts as found in the Bible.

Principle 10: We understand that the foundation of Christian Cognitive Behavioral Therapy is based upon the finished work of the cross of Jesus Christ.

Romans 5:8 (KJV)

8 But God commendeth his love toward us, in that, while we were yet sinners, Christ died for us.

John 3:16 (NKJV)

16 For God so loved the world that He gave His only begotten Son, that whoever believes in Him should not perish but have everlasting life.

Christian Cognitive Behavioral Therapy is founded in love, fueled by faith and grounded in forgiveness. Clinicians who employ CCBT are driven to give to their client's out of their love for Christ and their desire to see individuals healed, made whole and set free by the blood of Jesus.

The basis of CCBT is pulling down strongholds that are set up in our minds and making them come under arrest to the knowledge and obedience of Jesus Christ.

Before we move forward we have to identify certain life scriptures that will be the foundation for us to implement Christian Cognitive Behavioral Therapy. As a therapist, I often ask the client's that I work with to identify a life scripture. A life scripture is a scripture or multiple scriptures that relate to what you are going through. These are scriptures that feel like it was written specifically for you.

As stated CCBT is scriptural. We will now identify life scriptures that are the foundation for CCBT. The first one is one that has already been repeated and will be repeated throughout the book. The scripture found in I Corinthians 10 is the basis for all Christian Cognitive Behavioral Therapy. Let's read it again, I am going to put this scripture in a different translation since we already read this early.

2 Corinthians 10:5 (NIV)

5 We demolish arguments and every pretension that sets itself up against the knowledge of God, and we take captive every thought to make it obedient to Christ.

The KJV version says to cast down. Cast down is to throw (something) forcefully in a specified direction. It is also an act of throwing something forcefully. Demolish means to destroy, annihilate, overwhelmingly defeat, pull or knock down.

The secular world has coined this term thought stopping technique which is a principle found in the basic CBT. Yet again it originated from the bible.

According to Wikipedia thought stopping is a controversial cognitive intervention technique prescribed by therapists (psychologists and psychiatrists) with the goal of interrupting and removing problematic recurring thought patterns. The problem thought could be a worry, an obsession, an urge, an unwanted habit, etc. One approach is to command, yell, or mind scream "Stop!" whenever the unwanted thought recurs, and then think of a more positive or productive thought to replace it with. Another technique is to wear a rubber band on the wrist which the patient snaps to punish himself whenever the unwanted thought surfaces. Dismissing the thought at will as soon as it is noticed is another method.

Thought Stopping (n.d)
https://en.wikipedia.org/wiki/Thought_stopping. Retrieved on March 26, 2018.

Yet again before this ever became a thing, scripture tells us what to do with unhealthy thoughts. Going back to our CCBT principles it again proves that we can have mastery over our thoughts. I have had client's say that they can't control their thoughts, but you can. You can't always dictate a random thought that comes into your mind, you can, however, determine how long it stays and how it impacts you. If a random unhealthy thought comes into your mind and you quickly dismiss it or cast it down, then you have mastery over your thoughts. Yet if a fear thought comes into your mind and you let it stick and stay then it turns into an emotional, mental and unhealthy pattern in our lives. We will talk more about casting down unhealthy thoughts in another chapter.

Another life scripture that we must emphasize in Christian Cognitive Behavioral Therapy is our scriptures about meditating on the word of God.

Joshua 1:6-8 (NKJV)

6 Be strong and of good courage, for to this people you shall divide as an inheritance the land which I swore to their fathers to give them.

7 Only be strong and very courageous, that you may observe to do according to all the law which Moses My servant commanded you; do not turn from it to the right hand or to the left, that you may prosper wherever you go.

 8 This Book of the Law shall not depart from your mouth, but you shall meditate in it day and night, that you may observe to do according to all that is written in it. For then you will make your way prosperous, and then you will have good success.

A lot of unhealthy thinking that leads to depression and anxiety really has more to do with what we replay over and over in our minds. Ruminate means think deeply about something. Ruminate means to replay something or recycle something in our minds repeatedly. To ruminate is to meditate. Yet the scripture says in Joshua that we are to meditate. Most Christians have a problem with the word meditate because once again they have a secularized definition of meditation. Meditation is not sitting on the floor with our knees cross and your hands in mid-air trying to find inner peace.

NO   **YES!!!**

Notice one is trying to find inner peace inside of themselves the other is meditating on the word of God, which then brings the peace of God.

Notice the scripture tells us in Joshua to be strong and courageous. Be is an active word, it means an intentional decision. You must make an intentional decision to be strong and be courageous, then the scriptures tell us how we get to courageous and strong, and that is to observe the law of God, or the principles of God and then to meditate on God's word. The point is in Christ we don't find inner peace by stilling our minds, we find inner peace in God, through His son Jesus Christ. Meditating on the word of God is a key component of Christian Cognitive Behavioral Therapy.

Psalm 1:2 (NKJV)

2 But his delight is in the law of the Lord,

   And in His law he meditates day and night.

Psalm 77:6 (NKJV)

6 I call to remembrance my song in the night;

I meditate within my heart,

And my spirit makes diligent search.

Psalm 63:6 When I remember You on my bed, I meditate on You in the night watches.

Psalm 77:6 I call to remembrance my song in the night; I meditate within my heart, And my spirit makes diligent search.

Psalm 77:12 I will also meditate on all Your work, And talk of Your deeds.

Psalm 119:15 I will meditate on Your precepts, And contemplate Your ways.

Psalm 119:23 Princes also sit and speak against me, But Your servant meditates on Your statutes.

Psalm 119:27 Make me understand the way of Your precepts; So shall I meditate on Your wonderful works.

Psalm 119:48 My hands also I will lift up to Your commandments, Which I love, And I will meditate on Your statutes.

Psalm 119:78 Let the proud be ashamed, For they treated me wrongfully with falsehood; But I will meditate on Your precepts.

Psalm 119:148 My eyes are awake through the night watches, That I may meditate on Your word.

Psalm 143:5 I remember the days of old; I meditate on all Your works; I muse on the work of Your hands.

Psalm 145:5 I will meditate on the glorious splendor of Your majesty, And on Your wondrous works.

Isaiah 33:18 Your heart will meditate on terror: "Where is the scribe? Where is he who weighs? Where is he who counts the towers?"

Malachi 3:16 [A Book of Remembrance] Then those who feared the Lord spoke to one another, And the Lord listened and heard them; So a book of remembrance was written before Him For those who fear the Lord And who meditate on His name

Scriptural Meditations	
Meditate	Delight is in the law I meditate within my heart Meditate on Meditate within my heart Meditate on Your statutes. Meditate on all Your work, Meditate on Your precepts Meditate on the glorious splendor Meditate on His name

Scripture meditation is always focused on God. His wonderful works, His glorious name, His promises.

Our other life scripture is simple but profound, the scripture is found in Genesis 3:11, the scriptures begins with three simple words, "who told you?"

The foundation principle of Christian Cognitive Behavioral Therapy is that what we listen to and what we choose to believe is a direct relationship to what we achieve or not achieve. Your emotional and mental health is a direct correlation to what and who we allowed in our ear. In fact, if we took an honest review of when our lives and where our lives took a turn for the worst or for the better, there is a direct correlation between who we who we allowed to influence us. Who we allowed in our ear. My pastor from Maryland told us that when God wants to bless you He will send you somebody when the enemy wants to distract your purpose and destiny He will send a person to distract you. This is why we must teach our client's Christian stop thinking techniques, we have to teach our client's that thoughts only have influence over us based on what we allow. Let's read the scripture in its totality.

Genesis 3:11 (NKJV)

11 And He said, "Who told you that you were naked? Have you eaten from the tree of which I commanded you that you should not eat?"

We have to help our client to think about whose voice
they are listening to.

John 10:10 (KJV)

10 The thief cometh not, but for to steal, and to kill, and to destroy: I am come that they might have life, and that they might have it more abundantly.

This is not limited to our clients who have psychotic symptoms. We also include the clients who have reoccurring negative thoughts about themselves and the world that they live in. The scripture in John 10 is not limited to physical. The enemy comes to steal your purpose, kill your destiny and give you a defeated life. But God is saying I came to give you abundance. So, any thought not like God is from the enemy. Any thought of abundance is from God.

I hope you are getting excited about witnessing the power of God move through your client's. Christian Cognitive Behavioral Therapy is a wonderful intervention to see lives transformed and changed by the blood of Jesus.

Chapter 4

Challenging Thoughts and Faulty Thinking Patterns

2 Corinthians 10:5 (KJV)

5 Casting down imaginations, and every high thing that exalteth itself against the knowledge of God, and bringing into captivity every thought to the obedience of Christ;

We started with identifying faulty thinking patterns. What does faulty thinking mean? How do we know it is faulty? Where does faulty thinking come from?

Faulty means working badly or unreliable because of imperfections. Faulty thinking simply means errors in thinking. If a thought leads us to depression, worry, anxiety, self-defeat, self-loathing it can be defined as a faulty thought. Any thought that leads us to question and doubt the voice of God is considered a faulty thinking pattern. Faulty thoughts are always patterns and repeated habits of faulty thinking.

First let's start by identifying different types of faulty thinking patterns.

"1.) ALL-OR-NOTHING THINKING: You see things in black-and-white categories. If your performance falls short of perfect, you see yourself as a total failure.

2.) OVERGENERALIZATION: You see a single negative event as a never-ending pattern of defeat.

3.) MENTAL FILTER: You pick out a single negative detail and dwell on it exclusively so that your vision of all reality becomes darkened, like the drop of ink that discolors the entire beaker of water.

4.) DISQUALIFYING THE POSITIVE: You reject positive experiences by insisting they "don't count" for some reason or other. In this way, you can maintain a negative belief that is contradicted by your everyday experiences.

5.) JUMPING TO CONCLUSIONS: You make a negative interpretation even though there are no definite facts that convincingly support your conclusion.

A.) MIND READING: You arbitrarily conclude that someone is reacting negatively to you, and you don't bother to check this out.

B.) FORTUNE TELLING: You anticipate that things will turn out badly, and you feel convinced that your prediction is an already-established fact.

6.) MAGNIFICATION (CATASTROPHIZING) OR MINIMIZATION: You exaggerate the importance of things (such as your goof-up or someone else's achievement), or you inappropriately shrink things until they appear tiny (your own desirable qualities or other fellow's imperfections). This is also called the "binocular trick."

7.) EMOTIONAL REASONING: You assume that your negative emotions necessarily reflect the way things really are: "I feel it, therefore it must be true."

8.) SHOULD STATEMENTS: You try to motivate yourself with should and shouldn't as if you had to be whipped and punished before you could be expected to do anything. "Musts" and "oughts" are also offenders. The emotional consequences are guilt. When you direct should statement toward others, you feel anger, frustration, and resentment.

9.) LABELING AND MISLABELING: This is an extreme form of overgeneralization. Instead of describing your error, you attach a negative label to yourself. "I'm a loser." When someone else's behavior rubs you the wrong way, you attach a negative label to him" "He's a damn louse." Mislabeling involves describing an event with language that is highly colored and emotionally loaded.10.)

PERSONALIZATION: You see your self as the cause of some negative external event, which in fact you were not primarily responsible for."

 Burns, David D., MD. 1989. The Feeling Good Handbook. New York: William Morrow and Company).

Presumptuous	Readiness to presume or assume a conduct or thought, as by saying or doing something without right or permission. You assume that someone is doing something wrong, therefore you believe it to be true without evidence or facts to support.
Evil Foreboding	The act of one who forebodes; also :an omen, prediction, or presentiment especially of coming evil :portent. You believe something bad is going to happen without evidence.
Pessimistic	Tending to see the worst aspect of things or believe that the worst will happen. Questions peoples motives, inability to trust
Proud (prideful)	Having or showing arrogant superiority to and disdain of those one views as unworthy
False Humility	Thinking poorly of oneself, low self-esteem, feeling inferior. Tendency to be self-despising or to belittle oneself, to be self-deprecating around others, excessively modest, due to feeling inferior, useless, or unworthy
wicked (vein) imagination	A heart that plots evil, feet that race to do wrong, (NLT)
sowing discord	Their perverted hearts plot evil, and they constantly stir up trouble.
Wrath	extreme anger (chiefly used for humorous or rhetorical effect).
Gossip	casual or unconstrained conversation or reports about other people, typically involving details that are not confirmed as being true
Fear	an unpleasant emotion caused by the belief that someone or something is dangerous, likely to cause pain, or a threat.

Suspicious	having or showing a cautious distrust of someone or something.
Skeptical (skeptic)	not easily convinced; having doubts or reservations.

Each faulty thought pattern affects how we view ourselves and how we view God. Each thought patterns makes us question in a skeptic way. Faulty thinking is never a positive. You will find that often Christians try to spiritualize their negative thought patterns, for example, we don't call being suspicious a faulty thought pattern we call it using discernment. If using discernment causes you to think negative about everything and everyone you come in contact with it is not discernment. Faulty thinking impacts our faith. Faith and faulty thinking can't coexist together.

These thoughts come as subtle suggestions. My old Bishop use to say you have to watch the subtle suggestions of the enemy.

Remember the scripture we read several times in Genesis, satan came and questioned what God said. Eve then contemplated what was suggested to her.

A suggestion is a something that implies or indicates a certain fact or situation, an idea or plan put forward for consideration.

A suggestion is the psychological process by which one person guides the thoughts, feelings, or behavior of another person. Wikipedia.

The suggestion implies something. To imply means to strongly suggest the truth or existence without directly saying it. Let's go back to our scripture in Genesis.

Genesis 3:1-5 The Message (MSG)

1 The serpent was clever, more clever than any wild animal God had made. He spoke to the Woman: "Do I understand that God told you not to eat from any tree in the garden?"

2-3 The Woman said to the serpent, "Not at all. We can eat from the trees in the garden. It's only about the tree in the middle of the garden that God said, 'Don't eat from it; don't even touch it or you'll die.'"

4-5 The serpent told the Woman, "You won't die. God knows that the moment you eat from that tree, you'll see what's really going on. You'll be just like God, knowing everything, ranging all the way from good to evil."

Notice the serpent didn't flat out accuse God of not telling her the truth, he implied that God wasn't telling her the whole truth. He contradicted God, having her to believe a lie that she had to rethink or reconsider. I hope you are getting this.

So, if you have a client that says, "I wonder if something bad is going to happen when I leave my house?" They are not flat out saying, "I believe something bad is going to happen when I leave my house." The question that they are asking is implying.

This is the trick of the enemy, it is to have us question or doubt the voice of God. Therefore, it is so important for clinicians to know the word of God. If you don't know the word of God, you will not be able to effectively challenge faulty thoughts within the client.

This is the very nature of the enemy. It is the trick of the enemy to draw us away from God.

Revelation 12:9-11 (KJV)

9 And the **great dragon** was cast out, that old **serpent**, called the Devil, and Satan, which deceiveth the whole world: he was cast out into the earth, and his angels were cast out with him.

10 And I heard a loud voice saying in heaven, Now is come **salvation**, and **strength**, and the kingdom of our God, and the **power** of his Christ: for the **accuser** of our brethren is cast down, which **accused** them before our God day and night.

11 And they **overcame** him by the blood of the Lamb, and by the word of their **testimony**; and they loved not their lives unto the death.

Notice in the beginning satan just deceived one person himself, then he deceived two people Adam and Eve by the time we get to the end of the Bible in Revelations he has deceived the whole world. He started out a serpent and ended up a dragon. It teaches us his methodology, his relentless pursuit, to destroy. I want us to look at some key terms in revelations. A serpent is a snake, a giant reptile. A dragon is a full-grown reptile. It teaches us that what you feed will grow.

He started out a small snake and grew to…….

A big dragon

The tail two of the Cherokee Indian

An old Cherokee is teaching his grandson about life. "A fight is going on inside me," he said to the boy.

"It is a terrible fight and it is between two wolves. One is evil – he is anger, envy, sorrow, regret, greed, arrogance, self-pity, guilt, resentment, inferiority, lies, false pride, superiority, and ego." He continued, "The other is good – he is joy, peace, love, hope, serenity, humility, kindness, benevolence, empathy, generosity, truth, compassion, and faith. The same fight is going on inside you – and inside every other person, too."

The grandson thought about it for a minute and then asked his grandfather, "Which wolf will win?"

The old Cherokee simply replied, "The one you feed."

Two Wolves (n.d) http://www.virtuesforlife.com/two-wolves/ Retrieved on March 28, 2018.

There is no such thing as a little deception whatever you feed will grow. Notice the characteristics the Bible uses to describe the enemy.

Deceiver- someone who leads you to believe something that is not true. Fraud, liar, swindler, cheater. An accuser is a person who claims that someone has committed an offense or done something wrong. Yet look who the accuser accused, "the brethren." It means he who accuses anointed, people. Many people struggle with self-depreciating thoughts that come to their mind.

Yet look at the how the Bible describes the kingdom of God, salvation, strength, and power.

Salvation means preservation or deliverance from harm, ruin, or loss. Salvation also means deliverance from sin and its consequences, believed by Christians to be brought about by faith in Christ. It is hard to think God thoughts when He doesn't live in your heart.

Power- possession of control, authority, or influence over others.

Strength- power, force, energy, might mean the ability to exert effort.

In God is found the salvation, power, and strength, which then leads us to overcome. Overcome means the power to prevail.

The point is we can't change the circumstance of our birth, our parents, the past we can change how we see it. Perception will change your outlook if you allow. We have to teach our clients to restructure their thought patterns to focus on God. I said something earlier that I believe was quite profound it is worth repeating because I don't want us to gloss over this point.

I said, it is very difficult to think God thoughts when He doesn't live in your heart.

Romans 8:5-7 (NKJV)

5 For those who live according to the flesh set their minds on the things of the flesh, but those who live according to the Spirit, the things of the Spirit.

6 For to be carnally minded is death, but to be spiritually minded is life and peace.

7 Because the carnal mind is enmity against God; for it is not subject to the law of God, nor indeed can be.

According to scripture we cannot perceive or receive the things of God in our flesh, we must be spiritual. Ironically if a person is depressed, anxious, worried, full of rage, stressed, they are not operating in a spiritual mind, they are operated in a carnal mind.

That leads us to a very important point, as a Christian therapist, you will have different types of Christians in your practice. You will have people who identify as Christian, but they have no relationship with God. You will have doubting Christians, you will have Christians who have religious spirits, which is a major barrier to the effectiveness of CCBT. You will have Christians who are Christians by title, but their lifestyle is contrary to the word of God. You will have Christians who attend church, but their hearts are far from him. You will have Christians who are very legalistic. Advertising that you offer Christian mental health counseling doesn't mean you get people in your office that have an authentic relationship with God. The point is not to judge them. Yet it is important to note that as a Christian therapist there is a part of Christian Cognitive Behavioral Therapy where you will introduce Christ to them. You will introduce a Christ to them that they never knew and believe it or not that is perfectly fine.

I had a client working with me who is a prayer warrior. She loves God and has seen God turn her life around, yet she suffers from severe anxiety. In prayer, I was asked God how to help her. The Lord responded to me by saying, "when a person is affirmed (secure) in the Father's loves it cast out fear." The point is even though she loved God, she wasn't affirmed in His unconditional love towards her.

When we get our clients to refocus their thoughts, on God, that is when we will see transformation begin to happen in their lives.

I have a workbook Fight Fear With Faith, attached is a worksheet that I review with my client's. It starts the process of teaching them how to identify faulty thinking and reclaiming their thoughts to align with God.

Attacking Fear Thoughts

Philippians 4:8 (KJV)

8 Finally, brethren, whatsoever things are true, whatsoever things are honest, whatsoever things are just, whatsoever things are pure, whatsoever things are lovely, whatsoever things are of good report; if there be any virtue, and if there be any praise, think on these things

Is this thought true? Yes or No. What makes it true? Can I think different about it?

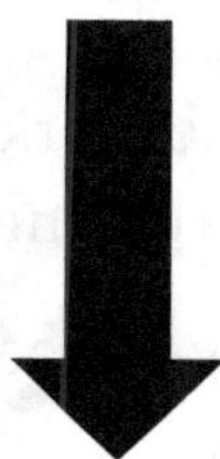

Is this thought just (pair), lovely? Does this thought make me feel good or bad? Why doesn't it make me feel good or bad? How can I rethink this thought to fit

Can I use this thought as a praise? Yes or no? Why not? In what ways can you praise yourself? In what ways can you praise God? Ex: "I thank you of God that I am fearfully and wonderfully made.

So, what do I do about fear thoughts??

2 Corinthians 10:5 (KJV)

5 Casting down imaginations, and every high thing that exalteth itself against the knowledge of God, and bringing into captivity every thought to the obedience of Christ;

1 John 4:18 (NKJV)

18 There is no fear in love; but perfect love casts out fear, because fear involves torment. But he who fears has not been made

Other ways we identify faulty thinking in the client is simply by identifying the fruit. Remember unhealthy thinking patterns are habitual, recurrent and most significant the works of the flesh.

Galatians 5:19-21 (NKJV)

19 Now the works of the flesh are evident, which are: adultery,[a] fornication, uncleanness, lewdness,

20 idolatry, sorcery, hatred, contentions, jealousies, outbursts of wrath, selfish ambitions, dissensions, heresies,

21 envy, murders,[b] drunkenness, revelries, and the like; of which I tell you beforehand, just as I also told you in time past, that those who practice such things will not inherit the kingdom of God

Sounds like the works of the flesh are thought patterns that we will see in the client. Ever meet with a client who needs anger management? Ever meet with the client who struggles with addictions? Ever meet with a client who struggles with bitterness? These are all works of the flesh.

James 3:14-16 (NKJV)

14 But if you have bitter envy and self-seeking in your hearts, do not boast and lie against the truth.

15 This wisdom does not descend from above, but is earthly, sensual, demonic.

16 For where envy and self-seeking exist, confusion and every evil thing are there.

What about the fearful?

Revelation 21:8 (KJV)

8 But the **fearful, and unbelieving,** and the abominable, and murderers, and whoremongers, and sorcerers, and idolaters, and all liars, shall have their part in the lake which burneth with fire and brimstone: which is the second death.

To be afraid is to believe in the wrong direction, to not believe what God has to say about you.

I know some of you are thinking, "ouch" that is a bit harsh, isn't it? As a therapist we are loving, kind, and giving. The indicators of unhealthy thinking patterns are not meant to be judgmental, but we must call it what it is. The reality is that many Christians struggle with fear, self-seeking motives, whatever. We as therapist are servants meant to bring the client from where they are to where they are supposed to be in Christ. We do it with the Father's love, but we also must call it what it is.

So how does scripture tell us to identify healthy thinking patterns? It is simply the fruit of the spirit.

Galatians 5:22-23 (KJV)

22 But the fruit of the Spirit is love, joy, peace, longsuffering, gentleness, goodness, faith,

23 Meekness, temperance: against such there is no law.

We are helping our client's shift from one mindset to another mindset.

Chapter 5

Treatment Planning and Goal Setting

Philippians 3:14

I press toward the mark for the prize of the high calling
of God in Christ Jesus

Your meeting with a client for the first time. What are
their reasons for initiating counseling? What do they
want to get out of coming to sessions? How do you
know when the goal has been met? Often client's will
have made tremendous progress, but they may not
recognize it because their situation may not have
changed. I had a client that was in an unhealthy
marriage. After meeting for a short time she is much
more confident. When we first started meeting she was
very depressed, anxious and presented with very poor
self-esteem. She is still working on her marriage and
struggles with second-guessing herself but is doing
much better. She is making great progress.

For some of you, this may come as a refresher or as a
review but for others that may be just beginning your
journal as a mental health clinician this will be vital
information. If you are already familiar with treatment
planning and goal setting please do not skip over this
chapter, this is still great information for you and you
never know you may just learn something new.

Before we get started the most important question that you may ask is can I write a clinical treatment plan for Christian Cognitive Behavioral Therapy? The answer is yes.

You simply document the clinical interactions and interventions with the client. Anything you do that doesn't fall in line with the clinical treatment of the client, you cannot consider mental health treatment although helpful. Examples include if you spent the entire session teaching the client about principles of prayer that is not a clinical interaction although extremely beneficial, not something you can consider mental health specific. However, if you spent time identifying faulty thinking patterns, and using ways to restructure them even if it is a biblical strategy that is still a clinical interaction because it falls under the CBT guidelines. I still document other events by using an NB note, (non- billable) so that I am reminded of what we did in our last session.

 You also must make sure that your goal is consistent with the mental health diagnosis and that the expected outcomes are measurable. To do that you must have a clear understanding of what the goal is and how you know when you reached it. You must also have a clear understanding of how to use the DSM 5. This book will not teach you how to use the DSM 5, as a mental health therapist you should be well versed in how to use this manual. You must also document progress, often the client has not reached the goal, but they have made progress.

Why is this important? Again, because there is a beginning, middle, and end to mental health counseling. Counseling done the right way brings a person to a place where they can come to terms with life's trauma and a place of healing. It doesn't get them to a place of perfection. One of my professors said we don't help get the client to be dependent on us, we get them to a place where they can be self-reliant and self-sufficient. She explained to us that there is a right way and a wrong to way to offer help. If you help someone so that they are dependent on you, you have done more harm than good.

This was in my undergraduate program and it wasn't a Christian college, but I took that as words of wisdom that I use to this day. I also applied that same concept to my spiritual journey in Christendom. Often, we see people having codependent relationships with their pastors and their Christian leaders. This is not God's will. Before you get offended in every book that I write I explain everything I say and prove it with scripture. The only one God expects us to depend on totally is Him. He sends Christian leaders and pastors to help us and to mold us. Scripture tells us this.

Romans 10:14-15 (NKJV)

14 How then shall they call on Him in whom they have not believed? And how shall they believe in Him of whom they have not heard? And how shall they hear without a preacher?

 15 And how shall they preach unless they are sent? As it is written:

"How beautiful are the feet of those who preach the gospel of peace,[a]

Who bring glad tidings of good things!"[b]

Yet when we look at the ministry of Jesus, He always prepared them to be effective ministers of the gospel, by mentoring them. He taught them how to pray, how to lay hands on the sick, how to hear from God. He didn't just do it for them, He trained them to develop their own relationship, then he sent them off to do the same in others. In fact, Jesus expressed frustration when the disciples couldn't do what he had trained and prepared them to do.

Matthew 17:14-18 (TLB)

14 When they arrived at the bottom of the hill, a huge crowd was waiting for them. A man came and knelt before Jesus and said,

15 "Sir, have mercy on my son, for he is mentally deranged and in great trouble, for he often falls into the fire or into the water;

 16 so I brought him to your disciples, but they couldn't cure him."

17 Jesus replied, "Oh, you stubborn, faithless people! How long shall I bear with you? Bring him here to me."

18 Then Jesus rebuked the demon in the boy and it left him, and from that moment the boy was well.

The point is we are not being used of God so that people are dependent upon us. We are vessels that God has chosen to bring people closer to Him. We don't become the voice of God for people, we lead them to His voice there is a difference. I once heard a minister say that if you are struggling to hear the voice of God, you need to find a personal prophet. No that is unscriptural. You must be planted in a word church, you must have your own relationship with God. You must understand that in your maturing in God there will be times when He speaks to you clearly and then there will be times when He appears silent. That is no time to seek man, it is a time to seek God. Pray, fast, seek His face and most importantly wait. God will speak in His timing, not yours. God never wants a man or a woman to replace a relationship with Him. You don't need a personal prophet, you need a personal relationship with

God. God will always confirm His word. Sometimes it may be from another leader, a prophet sometimes another pastor but He won't leave you to depend on a personal prophet. I attend an amazing church, I learn, I grow and most importantly I am taught the word of God. Still, that doesn't replace my own personal relationship with God. Often when my pastor teaches it is confirmation of what God spoke to me in my secret place. If it is not and I am learning something new, what he teaches me only ignites my passion for Jesus in such a way that I am motivated to go home and study further. There is a difference, his words although amazing leads me to a closer relationship with God. His words don't lead me to a closer relationship with him.

This is the same for why we are establishing goals, expected outcomes, and a plan.

Habakkuk 2:2 (NKJV)

The Just Live by Faith

2 Then the Lord answered me and said:

"Write the vision

And make it plain on tablets,

That he may run who reads it.

Before we go into resources let talk about what treatment goals should be and what they shouldn't be.

- Treatment goals should be clear and concise (specific)
- Treatment goals are what the consumer wants to get out of coming to the session (not the therapists)
- Treatment goals should be realistic and measurable. (We won't be able to get them to a place of perfection, we will get them to a place of clarity)
- Treatment goals for clinical notes must address the diagnosis FIRST. (remember this is still mental health counseling, not just Christian counseling alone that may not address a mental health diagnosis).

Now I am going to suggest some different resources that every therapist needs to have in their arsenal of tools to implement in counseling practice.

PracticePlanners
Arthur E. Jongsma, Jr., Series Editor
Includes DSM-5 Updates
FIFTH EDITION
The Complete
Adult Psychotherapy
TREATMENT PLANNER
WILEY

Practice Planners
FIFTH EDITION
The Adolescent
Psychotherapy
TREATMENT PLANNER
WILEY

PracticePlanners
FIFTH EDITION
The Child
Psychotherapy
TREATMENT PLANNER
WILEY

All the treatment planners are a must have. I am in no way affiliated with the authors but am simply giving you resources. I have used them for years. As a warning, the templates are not as measurable, but they give you a general idea, you can customize the suggested treatment goals to your specific client, in fact, I encourage you to do so.

The treatment plan is formulated after the initial evaluation is completed.

Some states call this a mental health evaluation, in North Carolina we call this the Comprehensive Clinical Assessment. If you are a therapist, you are aware of how to do these. If you are not a licensed therapist or have not been required to do these, you will find the information helpful. However, as a warning, I discourage individuals from implementing any form of mental health treatment if you are not a mental health therapist.

Even if you are in a church facility, you want to have some tools documenting the individuals presenting problems, concerns, and symptoms. We call this the medical record, now they are electronic, so the appropriate terms are EMR (Electronic Medical Record), other refer to this as an EHR (Electronic Health Record). This is very easy because everything is electronic. Even if you are not billing insurance, you still need this in your life. I don't do paper assessments. The two most popular that I am aware of are:

https://www.therapynotes.com/

https://www.theranest.com/

https://www.simplepractice.com

Note an EMR but be completed through a HIPPA compliant system. So, you shouldn't just formulate a tool through a basic word or excel document. Treatment and storage of an individual's records are serious!

Again, you can use these even for Christian counseling strategies. They are extremely helpful for keeping track of counselees, imputing paperwork, scheduling, and payments. You can also customize your counselee strategies to include different therapeutic interventions and other Christian counseling interventions. I cannot say enough about using them. They are relatively inexpensive, and for those who are mental health therapist who bills insurance, there is also a component that bills the insurance for you. If you don't bill insurance but still track payments, these tools are still useful.

Before we go further into the treatment plan let's briefly review examples of what your mental health evaluation will look like.

Mental Health Intake Form

Personal Information

Name: Date:
Address:
Phone: Email:
DOB: Sex:
Primary Physician: Phone:
Current Therapist: Phone:

Complaint

What is your major complaint?
Start Date: Have you previously suffered from this complaint?
Previous therapist(s) seen for complaint:
Previous treatment for complaint:
Aggravating Factors:
Relieving Factors:

Current Symptoms (Check All That Apply)

☐ Anxiety	☐ Appetite Issues	☐ Avoidance	☐ Crying Spells
☐ Depression	☐ Excessive Energy	☐ Fatigue	☐ Guilt
☐ Hallucinations	☐ Impulsivity	☐ Irritability	☐ Libido Changes
☐ Loss of Interest	☐ Panic Attacks	☐ Racing Thoughts	☐ Risky Activity
☐ Sleep Changes	☐ Suspiciousness	☐	☐

Medical History

Exercise Frequency: Exercise Type(s):
Allergies:
What medications are you currently using?
Previous diagnoses/mental health treatment:
Previously treated by:
Previous medications:
Dates treated:
Previous medical conditions:
Previous surgeries:

Family History

Were you adopted?   If yes, at what age?
How is your relationship with your mother?
How is your relationship with your father?
Siblings and their ages:
Are your parents married?
Did your parents divorce?   If yes, how old were you?
Did your parents remarry?   If yes, how old were you?
Who raised you?   Where did you grow up?
Family member medical conditions:
Family member mental conditions:
Treated with medication?
Medications:

Early Development

Where did you grow up?
How often did you move and where?
How old were you when you left home?

Mental Health Intake (n.d) Retrieved fromhttps://www.pinterest.com/explore/mental-health-assessment/ (n.d) October 30, 2017.

Mental Status Exam

Client Name				Date	
OBSERVATIONS					
Appearance	☐ Neat	☐ Disheveled	☐ Inappropriate	☐ Bizarre	☐ Other
Speech	☐ Normal	☐ Tangential	☐ Pressured	☐ Impoverished	☐ Other
Eye Contact	☐ Normal	☐ Intense	☐ Avoidant	☐ Other	
Motor Activity	☐ Normal	☐ Restless	☐ Tics	☐ Slowed	☐ Other
Affect	☐ Full	☐ Constricted	☐ Flat	☐ Labile	☐ Other
Comments:					
MOOD					
☐ Euthymic	☐ Anxious	☐ Angry	☐ Depressed	☐ Euphoric	☐ Irritable ☐ Other
Comments:					
COGNITION					
Orientation Impairment	☐ None	☐ Place	☐ Object	☐ Person	☐ Time
Memory Impairment	☐ None	☐ Short-Term	☐ Long-Term	☐ Other	
Attention	☐ Normal	☐ Distracted	☐ Other		
Comments:					
PERCEPTION					
Hallucinations	☐ None	☐ Auditory	☐ Visual	☐ Other	
Other	☐ None	☐ Derealization	☐ Depersonalization		
Comments:					
THOUGHTS					
Suicidality	☐ None	☐ Ideation	☐ Plan	☐ Intent	☐ Self-Harm
Homicidality	☐ None	☐ Aggressive	☐ Intent	☐ Plan	
Delusions	☐ None	☐ Grandiose	☐ Paranoid	☐ Religious	☐ Other
Comments:					
BEHAVIOR					
☐ Cooperative	☐ Guarded	☐ Hyperactive	☐ Agitated	☐ Paranoid	
☐ Stereotyped	☐ Aggressive	☐ Bizarre	☐ Withdrawn	☐ Other	
Comments:					
INSIGHT	☐ Good	☐ Fair	☐ Poor	Comments:	
JUDGMENT	☐ Good	☐ Fair	☐ Poor	Comments:	

Mental Health Status (n.d.) Retrieved from:
https://www.pinterest.com/pin/405957353883101655 October
30, 2017.

Christian Cognitive Behavioral Therapy

INTAKE ASSESSMENT

Client Name: DOB: Date of Intake:

Appearance	Mood/Affect	Behavior	Cognitions
WNL	WNL	WNL	WNL
Unkempt	Flat	Guarded	Loose Assoc.
Dirty	Depressed	Withdrawn	Scattered
Meticulous	Manic	Defensive	Blocked
Unusual	Anxious	Oppositional	Illogical
	Fearful	Hostile	Delusional
Speech	Irritable	Manipulative	Paranoid
WNL	Angry	Hyperactive	Hallucinations
Pressured	Labile	Impaired	Grandiose
Poverty of	Incongruent	Threatening	Obsessions
Impaired	Tearful	Impulsive	Dissociative

Insight/Judgment

Reliable informant   Yes ☐ No ☐
Knows needs help   Yes ☐ No ☐
Minimizes problems   Yes ☐ No ☐
Judgment   Good ☐ Fair ☐ Poor ☐

Sensorium

Oriented to time: Yes ☐ No ☐
Oriented to place   Yes ☐ No ☐
Oriented to person   Yes ☐ No ☐
Recent memory   Yes ☐ No ☐
Immediate recall   Yes ☐ No ☐

Statement of Clinical Impressions

Preliminary Diagnostic Impressions:

DSM Code   Diagnoses _______________________

Primary diagnosis as focus of treatment:

Personality factors:

Medical factors:

Psychosocial factors (V-codes):

Primary defense mechanisms:

Therapist's Signature: ___________________ Degree: ______ Title: ________ Date: ______

Intake Assessment (n.d) Retrieved from;
https://www.pinterest.com/pin/118008452712221724/ October
30, 2017.

COUNSELING INTAKE FORM

Note: This information is confidential.

Demographic Information:

Name:	Date:
Date of Birth:	Relationship Status:
Age:	SSN:
Gender: M / F	
Home/Mobile Phone:	Is it ok to leave a message for you at this number? Y / N
Work Phone:	Is it ok to leave a message for you at this number? Y / N
Email:	Is it ok to email you? Y / N
Mailing Address:	
Current Employer:	Position Title:
Current Occupational Status: (i.e., F/T, P/T, self-employed, student, returning to work):	
Emergency Contact Name & Relationship:	
Emergency Contact Phone:	
How were you referred?	If online, which website?

Behavior – circle any of the following behaviors that apply to you:

Overeat	Suicidal attempts	Can't keep a job	Take drugs	Compulsions
Insomnia	Vomiting	Smoke	Take too many risks	Odd behavior
Withdrawal	Lack of motivation	Drink too much	Nervous tics	Eating problems
Work too hard	Procrastination	Sleep disturbance	Crying	Impulsive reactions
Phobic avoidance	Outbursts of temper	Loss of control	Aggressive behavior	Concentration difficulties

Feelings – circle any of the following feelings that apply to you:

Angry	Guilty	Unhappy	Annoyed	Happy	Bored	Sad
Conflicted	Restless	Depressed	Regretful	Lonely	Anxious	Hopeless
Contented	Fearful	Hopeful	Excited	Panicky	Helpless	Optimistic
Energetic	Relaxed	Tense	Envious	Jealous	Others:_______	

Physical – circle any of the following symptoms that apply to you:

Headaches	Stomach trouble	Skin problems	Dizziness	Tics
Dry mouth	Palpitations	Fatigue	Burnping or itchy skin	Muscle spasms
Twitches	Chest pains	Tension	Back pain	Rapid heart beat
Sexual disturbances	Tremors	Unable to relax	Fainting spells	Blackouts
Bowel disturbances	Hear things	Excessive sweating	Tingling	Watery eyes
Visual disturbances	Numbness	Flushes	Hearing problems	Don't like being touched

Cherie May, M.Ed., LPC | 2109 Darlington Street, Birmingham, AL 35226 | P: 205-994-4563

Counseling Intake Form (n.d)
https://www.pinterest.com/pin/733383120540157290 Retrieved
on October 30, 2017

Again, for those of us who use the electronic medical records system, this will be in electronic form. You can customize based on your needs.

As a rule, there are certain questions you need to be answered and when meeting with the counselee at the initial session. Even though I use an EMR I still have a paper template because when I meet with the client for the first time I don't sit and type during the entire evaluation. The wonderful thing about being in private practice is that you can customize the client's experience to fit their needs. In my practice even though we are gathering the information I still make the first session more like a counseling session, so the intake is conversational. If you work at a group practice, for the most part, the expectation is that the first session is focused on gathering information. Now let's go back to our treatment planning and goal setting.

Sample Treatment Goals:

GOAL 1:

Chris will implement a parenting plan that promotes improved behavior in his son, as rated at least a 6 out of 10, where 10 is excellent.

OBJECTIVES:

Chris will make a list of the household rules.

Chris will make a list of rewards and consequences and will define how to enforce them.

Chris will present his new parenting plan to his son during a family meeting.

Chris will enforce rewards and consequences consistently and will monitor his progress in and out of session.

INTERVENTIONS:

The therapist will provide psychoeducation on positive parenting and will support Chris in developing a concrete parenting plan.

The therapist will provide materials for Chris to document the new house rules, rewards, and consequences system.

The therapist will monitor progress and check in with Chris weekly to ensure that Chris is implementing his plan consistently.

Treatment Plan (n.d) As found at;
https://www.goodtherapy.org/blog/psychpedia/treatme
nt-plan October 30, 2017.

Another question you may ask is what if the client is
not clear about what they want to get out of therapy.
Remember I said there is always a beginning, a middle
and an end to counseling. You must be clear about
what you are working on, how you know that
counselee is making progress, and what is the indicator
of the goal being met. Remember we start the
counseling sessions with the goal and end in mind.

PROBLEM(S): Problem behavior(s) to be decreased.	GOAL(S): Changes patient desires.	OBJECTIVE(S): Steps that will be taken to resolve problem behavior.	INTERVENTION(S): What therapist and patient do to aid patient in achieving objectives.
Anger Outbursts / Rage	Prevent physical and verbal explosions	1. Identify triggers 2. Identify strategies to manage anger 3. Decrease in verbal/physical outbursts	1. Daily diary card and review weekly 2. Skills training through weekly group 3. Chain analysis as needed 4. Role plays as needed 5. Family therapy as indicated 6. Phone coaching 7. Medication management 8. Individual therapy weekly

Counseling Plan Template (n.d) As found at
http://thebridgesummit.co/counseling-treatment-plan-
templateretrieved on October 30, 2017

Sometimes I reframe the question to something like, "tell me what it would look like for you if you weren't depressed?"

"What are some things that you love to do that depression may be preventing you from having a desire to do?"

"What were you like before the depression was a concern for you?"

If you ask the client, "what is your expected outcome?" They will look at you like with an "I don't know" uh response. This is important because as clinicians we are often used to our own way to speak that comes from our clinical or medical terminology based. When meeting with consumers we must meet them where they are? Open-ended questions.

For example, if a client tells me, "I use to love to be around my family and baked on Sundays for them, now I cry and don't want to be around anyone?" I use that to formulate the treatment goal.

Sample Treatment Goal
Goal 1: John Doe will be able to learn strategies of CCBT in order to be able to report a decrease in isolation, and increase in motivation AEB (as evidenced by)………

You can add to it your language but I would add something about spending time with family and baking more.

The other question you may have is what is the difference between the goal, objective, and intervention. The goal is the ending point, what we are working on towards. The objectives what the client does. What steps we are going to make to get to the goal. The interventions are the specific techniques or strategies to use, what the therapist does.

TREATMENT PLAN REVIEW

Client Name: _______________________________________ Case: ______________

Reopen Date: ______________ Inactive: ____________

Symptom rating for level of functioning change (scale 1-5; 1-mild, 3-moderate, 5-severe)

	Decrease in energy		Restlessness		Hopelessness		Excessive guilt
	Panic attacks		Cruelty		Loss of pleasure		Depressed mood
	Anxiety		Sleep disturbance		Withdrawn		Oppositional
	Poor concentration		Indecisive		Mood swings		Violation of rules
	Legal problems		Irritability		Helplessness		Eating disturbance
	Impulsivity		Worrying		Aggression/rage		Tearfulness
	Substance abuse		Ritualistic Behavior		Low self-esteem		Low motivation
	Other:					

Changes in Psychosocial/ Psychological level of distress: Greater: ______ Less: ____ None: ______

Changes in physical status: ____

Reports received/ Ancillary services documented: _____________________________

Treatment Plan: Progress toward /modification of goals and objectives, with estimated completion dates:

____
____
____
____
____
____
____

Treatment Plan Review (n.d) As found at; https://www.pinterest.com/janejackson513/goals-objectives-interventions/ Retrieved on October 30, 2017

Lastly, how do we keep track of the progress? SOAP not to be confused with the SOAP bible study method.

SOAP notes should include Subjective, Objective, Assessment, and Plan sections, hence the acronym SOAP.

Subjective: What we addressed in session today. The specific topic.

Objective: What course of action did we take?

Assessment: How did the counselee respond?

Plan: What will we work on in our next session.

SMART Goals Worksheet

This worksheet can be used to develop clearly defined, effective goals.

S	**Specific** What am I going to do? Why is this important to do at this time? What do I want to ultimately accomplish? How am I going to do it?
M	**Measurable** How will I know that I have reached my goal?
A	**Attainable** Can I see myself achieving this goal? Can I break it down into manageable pieces?
R	**Realistic** Is the goal too difficult to reach? Too easy?
T	**Timely** What is my target date for reaching my goal?

Smart Goals Worksheet (n.d) As found at;
https://www.pinterest.com/pin/560698222329176340, Retrieved
on October 30, 2017.

Another method is the pie method which is most common among mental health practitioners.

Problem: What problem did we address in session today?

Intervention: What intervention did we use today?

Effectiveness: How did the counselee respond? Include barriers, whether there was progress or not progress towards the goal.

Plan: What is the plan for the next session?

Christian Cognitive Behavioral Therapy

Client: Betty L Bieloski

Record Number: 2222

Medicaid ID: 021-53-8888K
DOB: 04/10/1962

1) Date of Service;
2) Identification of Recipient
3) Purpose of Contact
4) Description of Intervention
5) Effectiveness of the Intervention
6) Duration of Services
7) Signature and Position
(*Do not identify other clients in note.)

Date: 01/28/2007   **Service:** (90818) Individual Therapy (30 min)
Duration: 30 minutes   **Location:** 2 At Home / Regular Residence

Purpose:
 Demonstrate increased knowledge base of the predictable milestones of recovery process.

Intervention:
• Assist her in determining strongest triggers; money, people, places, things, etc., and ways to plan around them.
• Increase awareness of connection between AOD use and involvement with CJ system.
• Determine sources for non using friendships and work on friendship making skill development.

Effectiveness: Client appeared for a 50 minute individual treatment session as scheduled.
Betty was dressed appropriately and was in no apparent distress. She exhibited good organization of thoughts and communication. She understood the interview process and demonstrated adequate concentration and attention. She reports mood as happy and affect is congruent. Betty denies sleep or appetite disturbance at this time. She brainstormed alcohol free ways to meet potential friends, leading to discuss of self worth and realistic self appraisal of safety of activities where alcohol might be present. Client reestablishing ties with AA community. Client's increased self sufficiency, and partial attainment of treatment goals, suggest this intervention was effective.

Your Name Here, Degree(s)   Your Job Description Here

SERVICE NOTE B

Progress Notes Client (n.d) As found;
http://www.notebuilder.com/NoteTOC/ProgressNotes.htm
Retrieved on April 3, 2018

Common Intervention Terminology in Documentation

- Acknowledged attempts to...
- Actively listened to ct as...
- Addressed ct's concerns...
- Addressed worries/fears...
- Aided in developing insight...
- Allowed ct to ventilate...
- Amplified...
- Affirmed...
- Asked about...
- Assessed risk...
- Assessed for...
- Assigned task...
- Assisted ct in/with...
- Attempted to generalize...
- Built rapport by...
- Built trust through...
- Challenged beliefs/thoughts
- Clarified/Sought clarification...
- Commended...
- Connect comments about...
- Confronted...
- Contracted for...
- Cued...
- Deescalated...
- Developed a contingency plan...
- Developed behavioral program...
- Developed positive affirmations...
- Discussed...
- Directed/Redirected...
- Educated...
- Elicited...
- Encouraged...
- Encouraged verbalization...
- Engaged ct in play...

- Empathically responded...
- Established boundaries...
- Established connections between...
- Examined benefits/consequences...
- Explained...
- Explored...
- Explored self-defeating life patterns and beliefs
- Explored options...
- Evaluated...
- Facilitated...
- Focused on...
- Gave feedback...
- Guided...
- Helped ct develop...
- Helped ct to express anger constructively...
- Helped ct redefine...
- Highlighted consequences...
- Identified...
- Identified themes...
- Identified triggers...
- Increased awareness...
- Inquired about...
- Informed...
- Interpreted...
- Investigated...
- Led ct in practicing...
- Listed ct's...
- Modeled...
- Monitored...
- Normalized ct's feelings...
- Praised...
- Probed...
- Processed...
- Problem solved...
- Provided feedback...
- Provided a corrective social experience...

- Provided ct with unconditional positive regard...
- Questioned...
- Reassured...
- Redefined...
- Reflected...
- Reflected... (ND Play Therapy)
- Refocused...
- Reframed...
- Reinforced...
- Responded to...
- Restated...
- Reviewed...
- Reviewed limits...
- Recommended...
- Role played...
- Set limits...
- Summarized...
- Supported...
- Taught coping skill...
- Tracked... (ND PlayTherapy)
- Used directive comments to...
- Utilized desensitization...
- Utilized imagery/visualization...
- Utilized assertiveness training.
- Utilized relaxation training...
- Utilized humor...
- Utilized empathic understanding...
- Utilized silence...
- Validated ct's point...
- Verbalized...
- Worked on behavioral program

Common Interventions Terminology and Documentation (n.d) Retrieved from;
https://www.pinterest.com/pin/374502525234570323/?autologin=true April 3, 2018.

There are other forms that I have the client complete at the beginning of the session. If possible, I will email it to them and have them bring it to the first session.

Beginning (also known as the engagement session)

•Demographics Form

•Consents

•For those billing for mental health treatment verifying insurance.

•Statement of Faith Form

•Consent for Treatment Form

•For children, Child Custody Agreement Form

•Evaluation (identify why the counselee is seeking counseling, their history, when the problem began and how it is impacting them) (this is found in the electronic medical record)

•For mental health clinicians, you must use the DSM IV, use your diagnostic codes to be reimbursed by insurance for treatment rendered.

Review

When the evaluation is complete, we begin to formulate our goals for session called the treatment plan.

This is important because we must identify what the end goal is going to look like, at the beginning of the counseling session.

We must keep track of progress made. This is called a progress note, sometimes called a treatment note. There are different ways to track progress that includes S.O.A.P/ P.I.E/ S.M.A.R.T methods to name a few.

The EMR (Electronic Medical Record) is most helpful in the administrative side of counseling practice and helps us keep track of our counselees, our schedule, and the individuals progress.

Now let's get started with implementation.

Chapter 6

Implementation

Proverbs 20:5 (NKJV)

5 Counsel in the heart of man is like deep water,

But a man of understanding will draw it out.

How do you eat an elephant? I know crazy question but think about it. How do you eat an elephant? Answer: One bite at a time. Okay, okay I know we really don't eat elephants. At least I never heard of such. The elephant represents dealing with a huge task, assignment, project or in our case major emotional and mental health issue. You will have clients who have such a multitude of issues it may be hard to even discern where to begin. Unfortunately, in Christendom, most people don't come in for mental health treatment until things are extremely bad, because of the stigma associated with having a mental health concern. Sometimes when doing talks about the importance of treatment I don't use the words mental health I will say your emotional health. In fact, I just had a client who has severe issues going on, but she refused to go counseling for many years, because she was raised in the church, and was repeatedly told in church to have faith and pray on it. Well she prayed on it, believed, had faith and after many years still struggles with the same issues she has decided to get help.

It can feel overwhelming to you the therapist and for your clients when they have so many issues to address. Another reason why the treatment plan is so needed. It may feel overwhelming but everything in Christ is always possible. How do we know that? Because scripture tells us that all things are possible through Christ Jesus.

Matthew 19:26 (NKJV)

26 But Jesus looked at them and said to them, "With men this is impossible, but with God all things are possible."

Philippians 4:13 (NKJV)

13 I can do all things through Christ[a] who strengthens me.

Mark 11:23 (NKJV)

23 For assuredly, I say to you, whoever says to this mountain, 'Be removed and be cast into the sea,' and does not doubt in his heart, but believes that those things he says will be done, he will have whatever he says

These scriptures are significant because in secular counseling they don't believe in complete healing. For those who suffer from severe anxiety and depression, it can appear as if these are strongholds that will be there forever. For some severe anxiety is an insurmountable mountain in their lives. Yet, remember in Christian Cognitive Behavioral Therapy we must apply the word of God to our situation. Scripture says all things are possible through Christ Jesus then all things are possible through Christ Jesus. If scripture says we can move mountains, then we can move mountains. We can move mountains of anxiety, of fear, of worry, of depression. These are mountains that can be moved in Christ Jesus. This is significant because you will have clients who come from a secularized mentality on mental illness. They may not believe in complete healing. They may be reluctant to come. I have had many clients say, "I know I will never be completely free but I can get better." That is a secular mental health mentality. In Christianity, you can, and you will be free if you apply the principles of the word of God.

The strength of the healing has nothing to do with the effectiveness of the therapist rather the client's ability to apply the word of God to their situation, in the process and over time they will get better. Notice the word process and over time, meaning it is not an overnight thing but a process. The therapist is the servant leader. Those who are familiar with Christian healing and wholeness will often think of healing as when they go to the altar, and someone lays hands on them. We believe that when someone lays hands they are free forever never to address the issue again. Don't get me wrong I do believe in faith healings, but emotional and mental issues tend to heal over time and in the process, it is not a onetime event.

This is important because you will have Christians who come to you for counseling, they are guilt-ridden because they attend church regularly, they may be in ministry, in some cases pastors and ministers yet they still struggle with anxiety and depression. Experiencing depression and anxiety doesn't make you less than a Christian, it just means that you are human, with human frailties and there are underlying issues that need to be addressed in the presence of a spirit-led counselor.

We must implement Christian Cognitive Behavioral Therapy in steps and phases. Let's go back to our keyword here process. Process is a series of actions or steps taken to achieve a particular end.

I break down Christian Cognitive Behavioral Therapy in four phases:

Assess

Identify

Clarify

Restructure

A.I.C.R

This is where CCBT is very different from traditional CBT. The traditional way to implement CBT involves a lot of writing exercises, therapeutic homework and different strategies to identify faulty thinking patterns and automatic thinking patterns. Most therapists don't implement CBT the traditional way for this reason. We have found that many consumers don't want to be given tons of paperwork, some don't like to write, some don't want to analyze their thoughts to that extent. Most therapist will agree with me if you have ever attempted to implement CBT to it can be difficult to comprehend, because it simply doesn't work for the client in their everyday life. With multiple responsibilities, work, kids, life we therapist tend to simplify CBT for the average client. Trust me I have gone enough client's coming to the session, forgetting the therapeutic homework, not remembering to do it, we have to do something different. In fact, years ago when I started a depression group where we would implement basic CBT in group sessions. I got my group workbook. As I was reading through, the workbook, the documenting feelings and triggers worksheets were was so complicated that I couldn't understand it easily. I decided not to use it at all. The book has sat on my bookshelf for years, and I do mean years. If I can't figure it out why would I give it to my client to figure out?

The point is keep it simple, easy and understandable. I do give therapeutic homework, but it is simple.

The first phase that Assess:

I won't go into detail about assessment because we have already talked a great deal about that in the previous chapter. Your assessment consists of identifying the problem in a structured and consistent way. Therapist completes the assessment at the beginning of treatment. In North Carolina, we call it the comprehensive clinical assessment, some call it the psychological evaluation or the mental health assessment. After the assessment, you complete the treatment plan or the goals for treatment.

There are some questions that you want to hone in on, these are important to the process of treatment.

Things you want know is how does the client identify the problem? This is significant because how you see the problem and how the client may see the problem is different?

I had a client who came in for treatment. At our initial assessment, she identified the problem as having severe anxiety. She was also a Christian and felt guilty because she suffered from severe anxiety. As we completed the assessment it turns out she was also taking care of her grown children, in full-time pastoral ministry with her husband, had two adoptive children who had behavioral issues, recently missed a mortgage payment due to giving it to her adult children, was interviewing for a fulltime job, and taking care of her mother who had a severe mental illness. Her symptoms appeared to be anxiety and met the criteria for an anxiety disorder. Yet when as we talked it was clear that the source of her anxiety really was more related to being overwhelmed, not setting clear boundaries, not being able to say no and taking on too much responsibility. Are you seeing the difference? If we would have only addressed the anxiety we wouldn't have dealt with the real problem.

Other questions you will need to pose to the client is: How long has it been a problem? When did this start? What are their symptoms?

I have another series of teachings called Couches and Conversations about Inner Healing counseling. I encourage you to get those series of books. In inner healing, we deal with the root cause and go from there. Although CCBT deals with the root, it really focuses on symptoms. I tend to use a combination of Inner Healing counseling techniques and CCBT in session.

We then ask when did the problem start? Sometimes you are dealing with a root of something that began in childhood. I won't go into much detail because the Inner Healing work is quite extensive but when we are dealing with issues that are long term we have to look at the root causes. Again, pick up the series Couches and Conversations for further explanation.

We have the client identify the problem? When did they recognize it was a problem? What are the symptoms? How is the problem preventing them from living their best lives? For the goal planning, we identify how they would like their lives to be different as a result of participating in counseling.

Believe it or not, this is a biblical strategy. Let's consider scripture.

Mark 9:14-29 Living Bible (TLB)

14 At the bottom of the mountain they found a great crowd surrounding the other nine disciples, as some Jewish leaders argued with them.

15 The crowd watched Jesus in awe as he came toward them, and then ran to greet him.

16 "What's all the argument about?" he asked.

17 One of the men in the crowd spoke up and said, "Teacher, I brought my son for you to heal—he can't talk because he is possessed by a demon.

18 And whenever the demon is in control of him it dashes him to the ground and makes him foam at the mouth and grind his teeth and become rigid.[a] So I begged your disciples to cast out the demon, but they couldn't do it."

19 Jesus said to his disciples,[b] "Oh, what tiny faith you have;* how much longer must I be with you until you believe? How much longer must I be patient with you? Bring the boy to me."

20 So they brought the boy, but when he saw Jesus, the demon convulsed the child horribly, and he fell to the ground writhing and foaming at the mouth.

21 **"How long has he been this way?"** Jesus asked the father.

And he replied, "Since he was very small,

 22 and the demon often makes him fall into the fire or into water to kill him. Oh, have mercy on us and do something if you can."

23 "If I can?" Jesus asked. "Anything is possible if you have faith."

24 The father instantly replied, "I do have faith; oh, help me to have more!"

25 When Jesus saw the crowd was growing, he rebuked the demon.

"O demon of deafness and dumbness," he said, "I command you to come out of this child and enter him no more!"

26 Then the demon screamed terribly and convulsed the boy again and left him; and the boy lay there limp

and motionless, to all appearance dead. A murmur ran through the crowd—"He is dead."

27 But Jesus took him by the hand and helped him to his feet and he stood up and was all right!

28 Afterwards, when Jesus was alone in the house with his disciples, they asked him, "Why couldn't we cast that demon out?"

29 Jesus replied, "Cases like this require prayer."[c]

Just to clarify I am not suggesting that all mental illness is a demon. Nevertheless, I do want to point out that before Jesus laid hands on the boy to heal him He asked, "when did this begin?" The King James Version states, "And he asked his father, how long is it ago since this came unto him?"

The point is before the healing began Jesus assessed for when the symptoms first began.

If Jesus can do it so can we. Other things that are important to note is that some healings don't take place without prayer, the KJV version says prayer and fasting. Something the Lord has been dealing with me about I can pray but I need to do better at fasting regularly. The importance of this is that the therapist must have a prayer life and a fasting regimen so that real healing can take place.

Another thing to take into consideration is the client's faith journey. You will find that many individuals who identify as Christians may not know what a true definition of what Christianity is. Some view it as a religion, not as a relationship. Some think attending church means they are Christian. Some are Christian, but they never talk to God or don't consider Him as God who is concerned about them. We must use discernment in our approach. In whatever capacity you will introduce a Jesus to them that they have never known. For example, I had a client who is a Christian. Yet, she was always told that she was going to hell and was raised to be afraid of God even though she loves God and is a real Christian. How do you think that impacts her anxiety? Do you think she is prone to pray to a God she is afraid of? Although she is a Christian my duty is to introduce her to a loving Father, not the father that is going to send her to hell.

My point is just because someone identifies as a Christian doesn't mean they know God or His principles. We must therapeutically introduce them to a loving Father. That means meeting them where they are, not being preachy or offending them with your Christ. Remember Christianity is about the relationship, not religion.

The phase is to identify:

After we identify what happened we identify, what are the faulty thought patterns related to what happened?

Let's look at an example:

Sarah a 24-year-old woman suffered through sexual abuse as a child. We have identified the problem. Sarah's current symptoms are nightmares, flashbacks, difficulty trust, isolation, anxiety, guilt, shame. We have identified the symptoms, per our assessment phase. Still, now we have to identify her thought patterns related to the abuse?

Sarah believed that the abuse was her fault.

Sarah believed that she was unworthy, and ugly because of the abuse she suffered.

Again, for the identify phase of the treatment, we are only identifying the thought patterns. Remember we can't get free from what we don't acknowledge. This is the space for Sarah to be completely free and transparent. We don't want her to feel like because this is Christian counseling we are going to condemn her for feeling this way. We must identify the thoughts patterns that are unhealthy in order to get free.

The identifying phase means;

Identifying Automatic Thought and Unhealthy Thinking Patterns.

Let's go back and look at one of the CCBT worksheets.

What Happened That May Have Identified Triggered The Thoughts?	What Where My Thoughts Related To the Event?
Example: "I was brutally raped at the age of 12."	"I am no good." "It was my fault." "No one will ever love me."

Remember we aren't really giving interventions yet to reframe the thoughts, we are identifying them. Also, remember that I said we would have to make it simple for the client. You can complete the worksheet together with the client in the session, you can assign it has homework, or you can give it as a journaling exercise. Whatever way you choose to do it, keep it simple. I have some clients who love to journal their feelings, so this is perfect for them. Yet other clients can't stand writing their feelings, so you wouldn't give them a journaling exercise. In our counseling, we can be as structured or as non-structured as possible in order to curve the sessions to the client's preferences.

We can implement CCBT with teens as well. In some cases, teens may be reluctant to talk about their feelings or be truthful about how they really feel. In this case, I make it a game with teens, we do scenarios. I come up with scenarios that maybe like the teen's circumstance and then we discuss how the teen in the scenario may have felt. In some cases, I will turn it around on the teen and say, "you have similar concerns what part can you relate to this teen." If I get resistance that is okay. Remember the point is to build therapeutic trust with the client. We don't get to control when they trust us. We do have to submit to the process and meet them where they are. To make it fun for teens sometimes we will YouTube Dr. Phil Shows and watch brief episodes, I try to find an episode that is like their experience. As a warning, the episodes are between 5 and 10 minutes long. We can't dedicate an entire session to watching Dr. Phil, afterward we discuss the scenarios. Visual aids tend to work better with teens. In some cases, visual aids work well with adults as well. You will find for those who have experienced trauma in childhood, at times they may developmentally have stopped as well. You may have an adult client but cognitively they are 12 or 13 years old. Or cognitively they are 8 or 9 years old.

The next phase is to clarify:

Clarify means make (a statement or situation) less confused and more clearly comprehensible. After we identify the faulty thinking we must therapeutically help the client to identify this is faulty thinking. Just because you believe something to be true doesn't mean it is true. Nevertheless, we also have to do this in a non-judgmental, non-intrusive way. Remember this is not church this is therapy, we want to establish a therapeutic alliance. Therapeutic alliance simply means therapeutic trust.

Socratic questions are the term cognitive restructuring refers to the process of challenging, and changing, irrational thoughts. Socratic questioning is one technique to encourage this process. Use the Socratic Questioning worksheet alongside other CBT interventions to help your clients challenge irrational thoughts.

Socrative questioning goes like this, you first ask the question or identify the problem? Identify the thought related to the problem, then challenge the thought using Socratic questioning.

Socrative Thinking

Thoughts to be questioned:
What is the evidence for this thought? Against it?
Am I basing this thought-on fact, or on feelings?
Is this black and white, when reality it is more complicated?
Could I be misinterpreting the evidence? Am I making assumptions?
Might other people have different interpretations of this same situation? What are they?

Am I looking at all evidence, or just what supports my thoughts?
Could my thoughts be an exaggeration of what's true? Am I having thought out of habit, or do the facts support it?
Did someone pass this thought/belief to me? If so' are they reliable source?
Is my thought a likely scenario, or is it the worst case scenario?

Socrative Questions (n.d)
https://www.therapistaid.com/worksheets/socratic-questioning.pdf. Retrieved April 10, 2018.

Again, you can give the client this worksheet to complete for homework. Still remember we said we want to make it as least complicated for the client as possible. I use socratic question in conversation, to begin with. To be honest, I don't give them this exact worksheet, I am showing you this as an example of socratic questioning.

Let's go back to our scenario: Sarah identified that she was sexually assaulted, we identified the problem. Sarah identified symptoms. We then identified the unhealthy thought patterns. Sarah believes that the sexual assault was her fault.

Sarah, "I believe it was my fault because my parents told me to be home by 3:00 pm and I was walking home but I stopped at the convenient store to get a cola and that is where I met him."

Therapist, "had you stopped at the convenient store before Sarah?"

Sarah, "Yes plenty of times, my parents gave me extra change so I could get a snack and a cola after school."

Therapist, "so it was your regular routine to get a snack and cola after school?"

Sarah, "yes."

Therapist, "so I guess I don't understand how does that lead to the rape being your fault?"

Sarah, "well because I should have gone home and not stopped?"

Therapist, "yes but how did you know that day would be any different from the other times before when you stopped and got a cola?"

Sarah, "I didn't but you know …..it just that I….

Therapist, "Sarah I hear you, sometimes traumatic things happened to us and it is normal for us to think that maybe if you did something different you could have avoided what happened. But from what I hear you telling me is, on the day the rape happened you did what you normally do, which was to stop by the store and get something to drink before you went home. To me that doesn't sound like it was not your fault, you were doing your regular routine."

Are you seeing what I am doing? This is just an example and you can't really tell my tone because you are reading this instead of hearing me. My tone would be calm, warm and non-judgmental.

Socratic questioning is a specific way of asking question in a manner to get the client to rethink their assumptions about themselves and the world.

Remember assumptions are a thing that is accepted as true or as certain to happen, without proof.

The last phase is to restructure:

Restructure means to think different, it also means to organize differently. Restructure is another word for renovate. Renovate means to restore to a former better state. Most of our thoughts are imputed to us, we must rethink and restructure our thoughts to be like Christ.

This is so important that I have dedicated the entire next session on this phase.

Our next chapter will be dedicated to the final phase and that is how to restructure our thoughts to be in alignment with Christ.

Restructure happens after we identify the faulty thinking. We know it is faulty thinking because it is not in line with the word of God.

Other considerations, I said keep it simple however we still can assign therapeutic homework. We will talk more about this in our next chapter, but if you were raised in the church like I was you remember we would have Sunday school for the kids. Sunday school was where we learned about God. In Sunday school we also had a memory verse. One example of therapeutic homework within the context of therapy is to give the client one memory verse, I call them life verses. After the session, I may have a prepared memory verse for them to go over or meditate on for therapeutic homework.

Remember we are keeping it simple, I am not giving a lot of paperwork. Most client's get overwhelmed with paperwork, documenting every thought hour by hour, and identifying feelings. I can't emphasize this enough keep it simple. Sometimes I tell them to simply write it out on index cards and place it above the mirror.

Another tool you will find immensely helpful is YouTube. Sounds odd but we are living in a modern world where technology is at our feet.

I will have them listen to a preselected message on YouTube on their own time. I may have worksheets for them to complete, ask open-ended questions about what the speaker talked about. Basic questions include; What were your thoughts on the topic? Did you learn anything? If so what? We use open-ended questions, that make them think. Examples of preselected messages include;

Apostle Ivory Hopkins

•Any of his teachings on deliverance.

•Also, check out his teachings on marriage.

Pastor Steven Furtick of Elevation Church

•How to deal with disappointment.

•When anxiety attacks.

•Why am I so anxious?

Pastor Robert Morris of Gateway Church

Joyce Meyers (anything by Joyce Meyers)

Bill Johnson of Bethel Church

I use to give out teaching CD's but since most people have access to social media, I don't use them much anymore.

There so much more to learn on to our next chapter. Most people are not resistant to this therapeutic homework because it is simple and enjoyable. If you are going to create worksheets, keep it a one or two page minimum. Definitely not three or four pages. Keep the questions simple, open-ended, I generally have about five questions.

You don't need to wait to this phase to assign this homework, you can assign this homework at any stage, in fact, it helps to accelerate the healing process, plus you are teaching them how to develop their own spiritual life and work through their healing on their own.

Worksheet Example:

Talk Back To It

YouTube: Joyce Meyer Ministries: The Power Of Right Thinking.

Based on the teaching what are three benefits you learned about meditating on the word of God?

"The devil is talking to you, you might as well learn to talk back to _________________."

Identify what you learned about The Power Of Right Thinking: What can you do to put what you learned into practice?

Chapter 7:

Restructuring Our Thoughts To Be Like Christ

Philippians 2:5 (KJV)

5 Let this mind be in you, which was also in Christ Jesus:

Our journey as Christians is to be ever evolving and maturing into who we are supposed to be in Christ. We all are on a journey to get our minds and our thoughts to be like God. That is a part of our walk with Christ. If you have matured in Christ long enough you understand how we must be intentional about our relationship with Christ to live victorious lives.

I was recently at a women's meeting and I told the ladies we "we have to be intentional about our relationship with God?" Another woman asked, "what does it mean to be intentional about your relationship with God?" My response was to explain how some people identify as Christian, but they never talk to God, never spend time with Him, or they don't believe He is concerned about them. Too many God is in heaven and they are on earth, but He is not an intricate part of their lives. We are first teaching the client's how to be intentional about their relationship with God. As a warning if a person doesn't have a desire to have a relationship with God, it will be difficult to align their thoughts to be like God.

First, let's start by looking at how scripture can and will transform the mind, then we will go to simple implementation of CCBT in session.

First, our mind can be transformed and renewed by the word of God. When our thoughts change, our emotions, mental and spiritual health will only improve.

Romans 12:1-2 (KJV)

12 I beseech you therefore, brethren, by the mercies of God, that ye present your bodies a living sacrifice, holy, acceptable unto God, which is your reasonable service.

2 And be not conformed to this world: but be ye transformed by the renewing of your mind, that ye may prove what is that good, and acceptable, and perfect, will of God.

Let's dissect some of the wordage the scripture uses. Beseech means ask (someone) urgently and fervently to do something; implore; entreat.

The apostle Paul who wrote this text is telling us this transformation is extremely important. Present means to give as an offering, gift, to release to someone. Our bodies are our physical structure, that also includes our mind, our will, and our emotions. When I was a little girl growing up in the church we were taught about Romans 1 in terms of not intentionally sinning. Now that I have matured I understand the scripture more, I can present my entire self, mind, will, and emotions to God. Sometimes our hearts are full of fear, sometimes our minds are full of depression, but we must submit our entire self to God, not for Him to judge but for Him to transform our minds to be like Him.

1 Corinthians 6:19-20 (KJV)

19 What? know ye not that your body is the temple of the Holy Ghost which is in you, which ye have of God, and ye are not your own?

20 For ye are bought with a price: therefore glorify God in your body, and in your spirit, which are God's.

To be transformed to be like Christ we must submit our brokenness to Him. I use to think I had to submit a perfect body to God, but no God want's our brokenness. Once we submit our broken pieces to Him that is when transformation will take place. I am going to say this again because it is powerful, we must submit our brokenness to God, (mind, body, and spirit) in order for us to be transformed into what He has called us to be. This is how we transform into the glory (a reflection of God's nature)

Are you seeing the difference? Let me explain, what if you owned a home you paid a great price for. Then for some reason, you had to leave on a long journey, but again you still owned the home. While you are gone the house becomes abandoned, near ruin, decrepitated, and overrun. All the house needs are minor renovations and it will be worth way more than what you paid for it, plus you paid such a heavy price for the home it has sentimental value to you and you don't want to let it go.

What would you do?

My point we are worth so much more than a house. Our Father God loves us and paid a heavy price for it. He sent His son Jesus to die on the cross. We may have been abandoned, near ruin, abused, neglected, never the less we are loved. All we need is to be renovated, restored. We don't have to present a perfect self to God, all we must do is remind ourselves of who we belong to, and then present our broken vessel to God. He is the one that will restore us so that we reflect the glory of God. In Christian Cognitive Behavioral Therapy, self-will won't get us to wholeness our ability to relinquish control and give it to God is where the transformation takes place. We do have to be an active participant in the healing process because renovation and restoration is a process.

Let's go back and continue to our dissecting of Roman's 12.

Romans 12:1-2 (KJV)

12 I beseech you therefore, brethren, by the mercies of God, that ye present your bodies a living sacrifice, holy, acceptable unto God, which is your reasonable service.

2 And be not conformed to this world: but be ye transformed by the renewing of your mind, that ye may prove what is that good, and acceptable, and perfect, will of God.

Confirm mean to (of a person) behave according to socially acceptable conventions or standards. Confirm also means comply with rules, standards, or laws.

Transform means to make a thorough or dramatic change in the form, appearance, or character of. Transform also means, change, alter, convert, metamorphose, transfigure, transmute, mutate; More

When we make a decision to not conform to the past abuse, what society says we should be we then start the process transformation.

Look at the phases scripture gives us to transform our minds.

D-Don't Conform

T-Transform

R-Renew

These are three main principles we must identify in order to restructure thoughts. If scripture says, "don't conform." Then I must ask myself what am I conforming my mind to that is not in line with God?

We often have taken on a false identity, meaning we have conformed our mind to be something or someone God never created us to be.

We will talk about how to identify a false identity in our next scripture.

Identifying a false identity is not deep. If a person believes things like, "I am no good." That is a false identity. "I am unlovable." that is a false identity.

What do I need to transform to?

"more confidence, less fearful, boldness"

How do I renew?

This is where we use scripture? Scripture and relationship with Christ is the transformation power. We renew our minds with scripture. Look what scripture says about the power of the word.

Hebrews 4:12 (KJV)

12 For the word of God is quick, and powerful, and sharper than any twoedged sword, piercing even to the dividing asunder of soul and spirit, and of the joints and marrow, and is a discerner of the thoughts and intents of the heart.

So what does that mean?

Hebrews 4:12-14 Living Bible (TLB)

12 For whatever God says to us is full of living power: it is sharper than the sharpest dagger, cutting swift and deep into our innermost thoughts and desires with all their parts, exposing us for what we really are.

 13 He knows about everyone, everywhere. Everything about us is bare and wide open to the all-seeing eyes of our living God; nothing can be hidden from him to whom we must explain all that we have done.

14 But Jesus the Son of God is our great High Priest who has gone to heaven itself to help us; therefore let us never stop trusting him.

My pastor gave us a great example. He said how he was driving down the road a few weeks ago. As he was driving past the grave there was some kind of accident, and there were ambulance, and fire trucks driving past him in a rush. He said how no one in the grave jumped up to run for safety.

Scripture is not dead words. They aren't just affirmations we give you to help you believe in yourself. Scripture is alive.

Scripture is what takes us from the natural mind to the supernatural mind to be like Christ. Look what the scripture does first it is living power. It is not dead, dead works or dead affirmations. Scripture is alive.

Alive mean in existence; active: they kept hope alive. It is not just alive but living power. That means the more I get the word in my mind and heart it will transform me to be like Christ.

Look what else scripture does it cuts deep into our thoughts and desires. Why do you cut away something? I know I am asking a silly question but think about it. Why do you cut away something? Go ahead I am waiting to answer the question.

You cut away something you don't want, don't need. Cutaway means to discard. Discard means get rid of (someone or something) as no longer useful or desirable. Depression is something that is not useful or desirable. Anxiety, low self-esteem, anger, wrath are all things that we may suffer from that are not useful or desirable. Scripture is the supernatural power to cut away and discard it. Yet look what happens after it is cut away, scripture exposes us for who we really are.

Don't think to expose as a negative thought think about it as a positive.

1 Peter 2:9 Living Bible (TLB)

9 But you are not like that, for you have been chosen by God himself—you are priests of the King, you are holy and pure, you are God's very own—all this so that you may show to others how God called you out of the darkness into his wonderful light.

You are the child of the King. We think that God is going to expose our sin and shame but remember before we get to the exposing, we have already allowed the word to discard, cut away the undesirable, hidden things. What is left is who God has created us to be? This gets me excited.

Psalm 139:14 (NKJV)

14 I will praise You, for I am fearfully and wonderfully made;[a]

Marvelous are Your works,

And that my soul knows very well.

This is where we must teach the client the scripture meditation skills that we talked about earlier. We must also assist them in identifying scriptures to meditate on. Remember I talked about how we have many who identify as Christian but may not have a relationship with Christ. They may not know scripture.

We also don't want to overwhelm them, remember I said keep it simple. So how this looks in session is that I will give the individual the three scriptures to meditate on, I will also teach them how to meditate on the scripture. For example, I have a client who I met with yesterday, he suffers from severe PTSD, anxiety, and depression. I only focused on teaching him one coping skills yesterday after I introduced to him one principle. The one coping skill I mentioned was scripture meditation, in this session I gave him one scripture. The scripture that we just read in Psalms 139:14. I told him when he feels anxiety, and he feels a panic attack getting ready to come on. To place his hand on his heart and say out loud or to himself. "I praise you of God for I am fearfully and wonderfully made." I demonstrated it. I told him about fear thoughts that come as a false faith. I also talked about the trauma and how our brains remember what happened in the past and believe it will happen today or tomorrow again. We have to remind our brains that we are in a safe place, so I told him after he said that to say to God, "I thank you of God because I am safe in you, nothing is going to harm me."

I hope you understand what I am getting at. I gave him the principle. I gave him the strategy. I gave him one scripture and something simple that he can do. I actually demonstrated it for him. I don't expect him to transform overnight, but this is a strategy that if he implements will work overtime and in process.

We are slowly retraining the brain to think like Christ. Let's go back to our scripture we read earlier in Joshua.

Joshua 1:5-9 (NKJV)

5 No man shall be able to stand before you all the days of your life; as I was with Moses, so I will be with you. I will not leave you nor forsake you.

 6 Be strong and of good courage, for to this people you shall divide as an inheritance the land which I swore to their fathers to give them.

7 Only be strong and very courageous, that you may observe to do according to all the law which Moses My servant commanded you; do not turn from it to the right hand or to the left, that you may prosper wherever you go.

8 This Book of the Law shall not depart from your mouth, but you shall meditate in it day and night, that you may observe to do according to all that is written in it. For then you will make your way prosperous, and then you will have good success.

 9 Have I not commanded you? Be strong and of good courage; do not be afraid, nor be dismayed, for the Lord your God is with you wherever you go."

Courage means bold without fear. Courage also means the ability to do something that frightens you. We can say that we can feel fear, do it anyway and the fear will leave. Courage also means strength in the face of pain or grief. God was telling this to Joshua after Moses died and he was his predecessor. I wonder if Joshua felt afraid? Meditating on scripture bring us to strength, courage, prosperity. Prosperity doesn't always have to mean money it does successful, flourishing, or thriving condition. Let's look at a worksheet.

DTR Worksheet

Complete the following worksheet. Don't Conform?
What am conforming to that I need to let go of? What
do I need to transform to? What scripture can I use to
renew or restore my mind?

Don't Conform	Transform	Renew/Restore

Instructions: Take index, cards on one side put the problem on the other side write the problem to be meditated on.

Anxiety	2 Timothy 1:7 (KJV) 7 For God hath not given us the spirit of fear; but of power, and of love, and of a sound mind.
Anxiety	Psalm 91:1-2 (KJV) 1 He that dwelleth in the secret place of the most High shall abide under the shadow of the Almighty. 2 I will say of the Lord, He is my refuge and my fortress: my God; in him will I trust.
Anxiety	Matthew 6:34 (TLB) 34 "So don't be anxious about tomorrow. God will take care of your tomorrow too. Live one day at a time.[a]

We have to teach the client how to pray the scripture.
Praying the scripture is different from just reading it.
Pray the scripture is a response to the promises of God.
We also start with a thank you. You say the scripture
out loud and then the prayer response out loud.

Scripture	Prayer response:
1 John 4:18 Version (NKJV) 18 There is no fear in love; but perfect love casts out fear, because fear involves torment. But he who fears has not been made perfect in love.	"I thank you, Father, that I am loved by you. You are my God, therefore, I don't have to be afraid. Fear you must leave right now in the name of Jesus.
John 14:27 (KJV) 27 Peace I leave with you, my peace I give unto you: not as the world giveth, give I unto you. Let not your heart be troubled, neither let it be afraid.	"Thank you, Father God, that you have left me your peace, I don't have to be anxious or worried. I invite you Holy Spirit now to give me your peace. Heart, you don't be troubled, heart receives the peace of God."
1 Peter 5:7 (KJV) 7 Casting all your care upon him; for he careth for you.	"I thank you of God that you care for me, I don't have to worry about it. So heart and mind I cast this care on you.

Again we are keeping it simple. I don't give my client's a list of scripture. I do give therapeutic homework, I may only give them three scriptures to meditate on throughout the week, as the anxiety or depression comes. In our next session which more than likely is the next week, I will give them another three. I don't always hand out the worksheets. For some client's that it is appropriate for I do.

For example, the client I saw today is an avid reader and writer. She loves the worksheets, so I have given her worksheets and books to review. However, the client that I gave you an example about earlier, has a learning disability, is at times hard to understand words, so I wouldn't give him the worksheets to study on. The role play and demonstration was efficient enough. They both have similar backgrounds and the same mental health diagnosis.

There are other examples however I encourage you to be creative, make counseling fun. If you have a client that is into arts and crafts pull out those crayons and coloring books. I have one client who is diagnosed with dissociative identity disorder. (multiple personality disorder) Believe it or not that disorder is healable in Jesus. I have been working with her for years, she no longer meets the full criteria for the diagnosis, but she did three years ago when we first met.

The point is she is a gifted artist. Our sessions consist of coloring and art. She loves art and has now started bringing her own coloring pencils and art to the sessions. We talk about anxiety, depression, and severe trauma she experienced in the past but while she is talking we use art as a therapeutic to the tool.

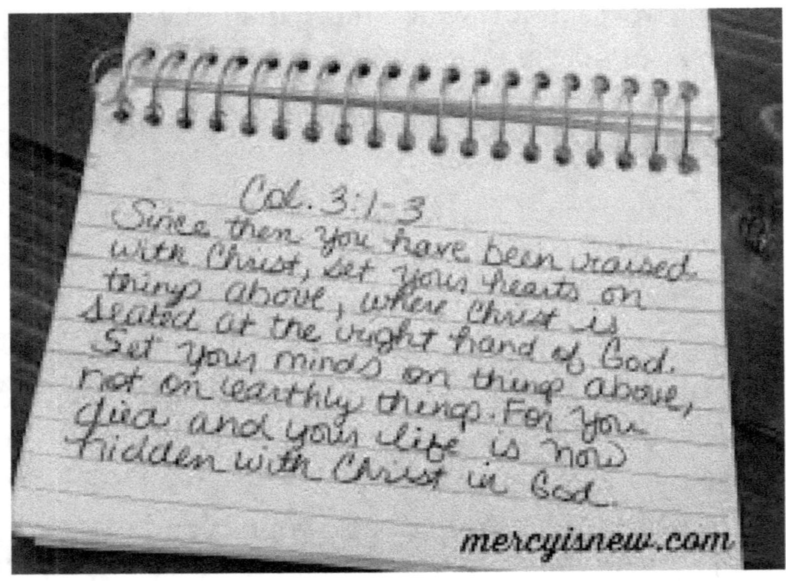

Crabtree, Candace (n.d) Praying The Scripture, Retrieved from; https://mercyisnew.com/praying-scriptures, Retrieved on April 10, 2018.

You can restructure the mind in different ways, music helps to meditate on scripture. One of my favorite songs is Safe In His Arms.

Lyrics

Because the Lord is my shepherd

I have everything I need

He lets me rest in the meadows grass

And He leads me besides the quiet stream

He restores my failing hands

And helps me to do what honors

That's why I'm safe

Safe in His arms

When the storm of life is raging

And the billows roll

So glad He shall hide me

Safe in His arms

So glad, He shall hide me

Safe in His arms

Songwriters: Darius Brooks

Safe in His Arms lyrics © Warner/Chappell Music, Inc

Imagine how playing that at least three times on repeat would help a person to reduce anxiety.

In one of my therapy sessions, we are going to come up with a playlist of songs to confront anxiety with. Again, be creative.

I have clients who feel guilty because they are Christian who struggles with anxiety and depression. They often feel less than Christian because of this. I have been asked how a person can be a strong Christian yet struggle with faith at the same time. The answer is found in the wheat and tare principle.

Matthew 13:24-30 (TLB)

24 Here is another illustration Jesus used: "The Kingdom of Heaven is like a farmer sowing good seed in his field;

25 but one night as he slept, his enemy came and sowed thistles among the wheat.

26 When the crop began to grow, the thistles grew too.

27 "The farmer's men came and told him, 'Sir, the field where you planted that choice seed is full of thistles!'

28 "'An enemy has done it,' he exclaimed.

"'Shall we pull out the thistles?' they asked.

29 "'No,' he replied. 'You'll hurt the wheat if you do.

30 Let both grow together until the harvest, and I will tell the reapers to sort out the thistles and burn them, and put the wheat in the barn.'

You see when God creates us He creates us whole, healthy, at peace and full of joy. We were created this way from the beginning just like Adam and Eve in the garden. What happens is the enemy comes along and plants snares. A snare is a trap. The snares comes as abuse, neglect, you name it. These wrong seeds are planted. Then they grow up in us along with our faith. God says don't just pull it out. Any gardener knows that you can't just pull out a snare it will damage the wheat, so He allows the trap to grow with the faith. At the end what the father will do is remove the snare, and keep the plant. It may help to tell the client that story as you will indeed come across that question. We are simple vessels of the Father used to help remove the snare.

Finally, this is where we use a biblically based principle. The world call this stop thought techniques.

Thought stopping is a cognitive intervention technique prescribed by therapists (psychologists and psychiatrists) with the goal of interrupting and removing problematic recurring thought patterns. The problem thought could be a worry, an obsession, an urge, an unwanted habit, etc. One approach is to command, yell, or mind scream "Stop!" whenever the unwanted thought recurs, and then think of a more positive or productive thought to replace it with. Another technique is to wear a rubber band on the wrist which the patient snaps to punish himself whenever the unwanted thought surfaces. Dismissing the thought at will as soon as it is noticed is another method.

Thought Stopping (n.d) Retrieved from
https://en.wikipedia.org/wiki/Thought_stopping. Retrieved on
April 19, 2018

Again, another concept that originated from the bible. I know we read this scripture before but let's read it again. You can never read the same scripture to many times.

2 Corinthians 10:5 (NKJV)

5 casting down arguments and every high thing that exalts itself against the knowledge of God, bringing every thought into captivity to the obedience of Christ,.

We stop the thought immediately. Cast means to through away violently. Replace it with scripture, the promises of God and something positive.

Philippians 4:8-9 (KJV)

8 Finally, brethren, whatsoever things are true, whatsoever things are honest, whatsoever things are just, whatsoever things are pure, whatsoever things are lovely, whatsoever things are of good report; if there be any virtue, and if there be any praise, think on these things.

9 Those things, which ye have both learned, and received, and heard, and seen in me, do: and the God of peace shall be with you.

Look what happens when we implement the biblical CBT stop thought techniques. It says the peace of God will come. Ironically, we are teaching them the clients words of life as found in the bible, they are responsible to learn (seek knowledge) receive and hear (intentionally listen to the instructions) and implement. Then the peace of God comes.

Chapter 8

Identifying A False Identity

Psalm 100:3 (NKJV)

3 Know that the Lord, He is God;

It is He who has made us, and not we ourselves;[a]

We are His people and the sheep of His pasture.

God created our identity, God framed our identity and formed our identity to be like Him. The truth of the matter is when a person isn't clear about who they are in God, they have taken on a false identity. When we begin to restructure our thoughts to be like God, we then begin to declare His promises. We also then begin to understand who we were created to be. We must reclaim our identity in God. It is important to note that in the beginning, God gave man authority, power, dominion and responsibility to tend to the earth that He created.

God never gave man permission, authority or power to change his or her own identity. When God created us, He created us in His image and in His likeness.

Genesis 1:27 (KJV)

27 So God created man in his own image, in the image of God created he him; male and female created he them.

God made them man and female. God never gave man permission to recreate who He had created them to be. So, it is to this day, therefore you can have as many operations as you want, your DNA will always be in line with what God has created you to be. You are either male or female based on how God created you be. You can claim to be transgender, gender neutral, not go by gender laws, asexual, whatever you call it in God's eyes you are either male or female. No, I am not a homophobic person I am just stating the facts as found in the word of God.

Believe it or not, everyone has experienced an identity crisis, it may not have been to that extreme, but you have experienced an identity crisis. An identity crisis is a period of uncertainty and confusion in which a person's sense of identity becomes insecure, typically due to a change in their expected aims or roles in society.

The truth of the matter is when you are uncertain about yourself, you have an issue with your identity. If you have looked in the mirror and told yourself, you were to fat, too skinny, too dark, to light, too many freckles, not enough hair whatever this is an identity issue.

Where do identity problems come from? They always come from following another voice that is not in line with the word of God. It happened in the beginning. Let's go back to the scripture we read earlier in Genesis when Eve followed another voice.

Genesis 3:10-11 Living Bible (TLB)

10 And Adam replied, "I heard you coming and didn't want you to see me naked. So I hid."

11 "Who told you you were naked?" the Lord God asked. "Have you eaten fruit from the tree I warned you about?"

We all know the story, God told Adam and Eve not to eat of the tree of good and evil, Eve did then Adam followed. They were deceived by satan. As a result, they were kicked out of their rightful place in the garden of Eden.

The point is when we struggle internally with our identity, with fear, with self-doubt and self-hatred it really has to with us following another voice that is contrary to the voice of God. Establishing a relationship with God and learning to love and listen to Him puts us back in right standing. It also helps us to follow His voice and to trust what He has to say about us.

John 10:27 (KJV)

27 My sheep hear my voice, and I know them, and they follow me:

This relates to Christian behavioral therapy because we must show our client's how they have embraced the false identity of fear or doubt. We must then show them how to restructure their thoughts to be like God. Yet we also must be able to understand what the characteristics are of someone who has embraced a false identity. This is not an all-inclusive list and in no particular order

The first identity crisis that we will discuss is imposter syndrome:

Impostor syndrome (also known as impostor phenomenon, fraud syndrome or the impostor experience) is a concept describing individuals who are marked by an inability to internalize their accomplishments and have a persistent fear of being exposed as a "fraud".

Imposter Syndrome (n.d) https://en.wikipedia.org/wiki/Impostor_syndrome. Retrieved April 15, 2018,

I can remember very well for many years of my life struggling with imposter syndrome. For years, I thought I wasn't good enough, wasn't smart of enough these were all lies from the enemy that I chose to believe as truth. I remember my first week at Howard University, I had just gotten excepted into graduate school. The first week of orientation, I sat there with all the other students, all of them at the same place as I, all of us wanting a career in the helping field. Yet I felt like I didn't belong there I felt like I had gotten excepted on a whim by some mistake or stroke of luck. I certainly didn't go in there thinking I would succeed. Thank God for deliverance. Imposture syndrome impacts many people, even people who are successful, that many people look up to. They secretly believe they don't belong and at that their success is not warranted, even though they have the blood, sweat, and tears of the work they put in. Imposture syndrome is a false identity. How do we know this, because we must compare this identity to the word of God?

Deuteronomy 28:13 (TLB)

13 If you will only listen and obey the commandments of the Lord your God that I am giving you today, he will make you the head and not the tail, and you shall always have the upper hand.

Head means at the top, success in every area of your life, having the upper hands. Yet notice that the only criteria for being the head are to listen and obey. To believe that you are the head that God says you are, you must believe it. In order to listen, you must believe and obey. Most people won't obey what they don't believe particularly when they aren't forced to.

I hope you are seeing how this relates to relinquishing a false identity and embracing what God has to say about you.

The next false identity we will discuss next is a victim mentality.

A victim mentality -- in other words, if you feel powerless to affect your circumstances -- you are likely to feel that the world is "doing it" to you and that there is nothing you ... Victims are, by definition, people who do not acknowledge responsibility for their actions and who blame outside forces.

Do You Have 'Victim Mentality'? What To Do About It (2010, Dec 18) https://www.huffingtonpost.com/morty-lefkoe/victim-mentality_b_794628.html Retrieved April 15, 2018

When a person has a victim mentality their conflicts with others are always someone else's fault. I had a client who always had a conflict with someone. She would come to our weekly sessions and go down the list of all the things wrong and some kind of issue she had with someone else. She would always end with an "I mind my own business, but people are so ignorant." Yet, when I listened to the story the only common denominator in every event was her. Let's look at an example of a victim mentality.

After Adam and Eve followed another voice, let's look at their response. This is a great example of the victim mentality.

Genesis 3:12-14 Living Bible (TLB)

12 "Yes," Adam admitted, "but it was the woman you gave me who brought me some, and I ate it."

13 Then the Lord God asked the woman, "How could you do such a thing?"

"The serpent tricked me," she replied.

14 So the Lord God said to the serpent, "This is your punishment: You are singled out from among all the domestic and wild animals of the whole earth—to be cursed. You shall grovel in the dust as long as you live, crawling along on your belly.

So, Adam's response was, "it was the woman that you gave me." He was blaming Eve and then God. Then Eve is in the hot seat and she blames the serpent. No one took responsibility. The truth is Adam observed Eve eating he didn't stop her and he certainly wasn't forced to eat. Yes, the serpent deceived Eve but he didn't force her to eat either, she chose to listen to his voice.

This is a victim mentality. No one takes responsibility it is always someone else's fault. This is very important when you implement CCBT with couples.

THE
BLAME
GAME

Neither individual wants to take responsibility for the way the marriage is going, rather they want to point fingers at each other. One intervention I have them to do is to explain what they each need to work on in the marriage and what they would like the other to work on. You would be surprised many have a list of things that they want their spouse to improve upon but have difficulty with what they need to work on. Marriage won't work if you keep up the blame game.

Creflo Dollar taught a message on marriage called, Deliverance from Self Centeredness in Marriage Relationships. He is quoted saying, "How your spouse treats you is none of your business, your business is how you treat your spouse."

Of course, this does not apply to extreme cases such as abusive relationships. A person will never grow with a victim mentality. How does this contradict the word of God? Because you have to admit where you are wrong in order for God to heal you. You can't grow or have a healthy relationship with God or others playing the blame game.

1 John 1:9 Living Bible (TLB)

9 But if we confess our sins to him,[a] he can be depended on to forgive us and to cleanse us from every wrong. And it is perfectly proper for God to do this for us because Christ died to wash away our sins.

Sometimes you just must humble yourself and admit you were wrong simple as that.

Another false identity presents as learned helplessness. Learned helplessness is similar to a victim mentality. The difference is when a person has victim mentality they believe that others are attacking them. When an individual experiences learned helplessness, they believe that they have no power to change their circumstance.

Learned helplessness also is present in codependent relationships. It is where an individual's life, self-worth, and identity is so wrapped up in another person, they have no sense of self and cannot make a decision or have an identity outside of that person.

Learned helplessness is a condition in which a person suffers from a sense of powerlessness, arising from a traumatic event or persistent failure to succeed. It is thought to be one of the underlying causes of depression.

Learned Helplessness (n.d)
https://en.wikipedia.org/wiki/Learned_helplessness. Retrieved on April 15, 2018

Learned helplessness presents in relationships in the following ways.

Giving your power over to someone else, for them to control, manipulate, and dominate you as they please.

Your happiness is defined by someone else's definition

" I would be happy but, he or she won't let me."

Your opinions, thoughts, and feeling don't matter.

Walking on eggshells

Second guess yourself, at the suggestion of another.

Feeling powerless at the hands of others.

Whenever someone tells you to stand up for yourself, you respond with a yeah but… and the yeah but…. always has something to do with whether someone else will respond negatively to your request to be treated respectfully.

How do we know that learned helplessness is contrary to our identity in God?

Philippians 4:13 (NKJV)

13 I can do **all** things through Christ[a] who strengthens me.

Notice the word all things. You can't say, "I can't do it" when you understand who you are in Christ.

What is learned helplessness in relationships?

1 Corinthians 15:33 King James Version (KJV)

33 Be not deceived: evil communications corrupt good manners.

2 Corinthians 6:14 King James Version (KJV)

14 Be ye not unequally yoked together with unbelievers: for what fellowship hath righteousness with unrighteousness? and what communion hath light with darkness?

2 Corinthians 6:17-18 (KJV)

17 Wherefore come out from among them, and be ye separate, saith the Lord, and touch not the unclean thing; and I will receive you.

18 And will be a Father unto you, and ye shall be my sons and daughters, saith the Lord Almighty.

Some things you just have to let go of people. A lot of our healing would take place if we just stopped aligning ourselves with people who don't believe in us or who don't see our value. When we as Christians read the text in 2 Corinthians we think of not being yoked with non-Christians, but the Bible clearly says, unbelievers. A person can identify as a Christian and still be an unbeliever.

If they don't believe in your worth and value as a person, they are an unbeliever. If they don't want, you to succeed they are an unbeliever. If they keep telling you what you can't do or achieve they are an unbeliever. It doesn't matter how Christian they are.

I once counseled a person who was married to a minister. The minister was always putting her down.

Yes, he was a minister but still an unbeliever. This is an example of taking on a false identity simply because of who we allow in our ear.

The next false identity that we will discuss is the orphan spirit.

When a person has the fruit of rejection, they are not clear about their identity with God.

Think about what an orphan is. An orphan is a child who has no parents, or their parents are dead. Imagine going through life feeling as if no one wants you; you are not loved. The individual may not be an orphan naturally, but they have an orphan spirit. When we counsel others, we must assist them in understanding that God loves them, that they have His very nature. They belong to Him.

An orphan spirit is someone who doesn't feel as though they belong to anyone. They feel unwanted and unloved.

In 2012 article by Prophet Helen Calder she identifies four characteristics of a person who has an orphan spirit.

1. Competing and Needing to Stand Out

Spiritual orphans do not feel accepted and feel the need to prove their worth.

2. Isolation or Independence

Deep down the orphan does not feel as though he or she belongs to the family. Suffering a sense of abandonment, the instinct of an orphan is to go it alone.

3. Fear and Insecurity

The spiritual orphan is unsure of his or her place in the family. Orphans also feel uncovered and unprotected—therefore their instinct is to protect themselves and their position.

4. Performance-Orientation

The spiritual orphan feels rejected—therefore believing that he or she must compensate by working hard or performing well in order to be recognized.

4 Symptoms of the Orphan Spirit in Church Life. (2012 September 17). https://www.enlivenpublishing.com/blog/2012/09/17/4-symptoms-of-the-orphan-spirit-in-church-life/ Retrieved on April 15, 2018

So what answers do we need to find in the word of God to heal the orphan spirit?

Romans 8:15 (NKJV)

15 For you did not receive the spirit of bondage again to fear, but you received the Spirit of adoption by whom we cry out, "Abba, Father."

We have all been adopted. Yes, that's right adopted. I received a call from a young lady a few years back she wanted to schedule for counseling. When we discussed further her purpose for seeking counseling, she reported that she was struggling with feeling abandoned and not wanted because she had been adopted. She felt the abandonment from her birth parents even though her adoptive parents had chosen her.

This feeling of abandonment is not uncommon for individuals who have been adopted. Even if they have never met their birth parents, there is this underlying thought that focuses on being let go of by their birth parents. I still want you to hold on to the fact that you have been adopted. We all have been adopted. We must declare this thought as a badge of honor. First, let's explore what it means to be adopted. Adopted means to choose or take as one's own; make one's own by selection or assent.

When you have been adopted, you have been specifically selected, chosen. Look at the scripture we read at the beginning of the chapter.

Romans 8:15 (TLB)

15 And so we should not be like cringing, fearful slaves, but we should behave like God's very own children, adopted into the bosom of his family, and calling to him, "Father, Father."

Psalm 27:10 (TLB)

10 For if my father and mother should abandon me, you would welcome and comfort me.

So, when you look at it from that perspective adoption is not a bad thing it is a good thing. Many look at adoption from the negative connotation. The wonderful thing about it is something supernatural happens when we embrace the father's adoption.

Romans 11:17 (TLB)

17 But some of these branches from Abraham's tree, some of the Jews, have been broken off. And you Gentiles who were branches from, we might say, a wild olive tree, were grafted in. So now you, too, receive the blessing God has promised Abraham and his children, sharing in God's rich nourishment of his special olive tree.

Graft means to join by such union; it means to be molded into.

When God adopts you, you are not the outcast; you are not the adopted child, you are His, you are the chosen one. The more you grow in Him and continue in your relationship with Him, you begin to take on His nature, you then take on His DNA, you have His blood type. This is something that doesn't happen with natural children but adopted children. You may look like your adoptive parents, you may even start sounding like your adoptive parents because the more you spend time with someone in a relationship you begin to take each other characteristics. Though, if you have the opposite blood type, it will never change. You will never have their DNA, not so with God.

My point is if we are going to walk as a royal child of God and teach our client's how to walk in a children of God we must embrace His adoption. We are really sons and daughters of God.

1 Peter 2:9 Living Bible (TLB)

9 But you are not like that, for you have been chosen by God himself—you are priests of the King, you are holy and pure, you are God's very own—all this so that you may show to others how God called you out of the darkness into his wonderful light.

1 Peter 2:9 King James Version (KJV)

9 But ye are a chosen generation, a royal priesthood, an holy nation, a peculiar people; that ye should shew forth the praises of him who hath called you out of darkness into his marvellous light;

Ever felt stranger, like you were the odd one out like you didn't fit? Well get encouraged you are in good company. Your Abba created you that way.

Ever been rejected, overlooked, ignored, be confident your Abba Father made you that way for a reason.

1 Corinthians 1:27-30 Living Bible (TLB)

27 Instead, God has deliberately chosen to use ideas the world considers foolish and of little worth in order to shame those people considered by the world as wise and great.

28 He has chosen a plan despised by the world, counted as nothing at all, and used it to bring down to nothing those the world considers great,

29 so that no one anywhere can ever brag in the presence of God.

30 For it is from God alone that you have your life through Christ Jesus. He showed us God's plan of salvation; he was the one who made us acceptable to God; he made us pure and holy[a] and gave himself to purchase our salvation.

We are sons and daughters of the highest God.

Another false identity is the performance-driven person. These are individuals who are driven to succeed in order to earn love, acceptance. Joyce

Meyer's coined the term approval addiction. Some also call this works of the flesh.

Romans 4:1-5 Living Bible (TLB)

4 1-2 Abraham was, humanly speaking, the founder of our Jewish nation. What were his experiences concerning this question of being saved by faith? Was it because of his good deeds that God accepted him? If so, then he would have something to boast about. But from God's point of view Abraham had no basis at all for pride.

3 For the Scriptures tell us Abraham believed God, and that is why God canceled his sins and declared him "not guilty."

4-5 But didn't he earn his right to heaven by all the good things he did? No, for being saved is a gift; if a person could earn it by being good, then it wouldn't be free—but it is! It is given to those who do not work for it. For God declares sinners to be good in his sight if they have faith in Christ to save them from God's wrath.[a]

The point is we don't have to earn God's love we have to believe and receive it through faith. If we are assured of God's love for us we don't have to prove ourselves to man, we have already been approved by God. God and you are the majority.

Wrong motives, believe it or not, is a sign of being motivated by a false identity. Motive simply is the reason why you do what you do. The motive is also a reason for doing something, especially one that is hidden or not obvious. Sometimes we want things from God, but we have wrong motives.

Acts 8:18-21 (KJV)

18 And when Simon saw that through laying on of the apostles' hands the Holy Ghost was given, he offered them money,

19 Saying, Give me also this power, that on whomsoever I lay hands, he may receive the Holy Ghost.

20 But Peter said unto him, Thy money perish with thee, because thou hast thought that the gift of God may be purchased with money.

21 Thou hast neither part nor lot in this matter: for thy heart is not right in the sight of God.

We all want the power of God to manifest in our lives, but Barnabas thought he could buy the gift of God. I don't know about you, but I have heard in church that all I needed to do was sow a seed of x amount and my purpose and destiny would manifest. If it were only easy but it is not. You know someone has false motives because the reason why they are doing something is not to honor God or to help people, rather to somehow enhance themselves.

Examples of this would be a person who starts a ministry, so they can get accolades from man or prove to people that rejected them that they were really somebody important. Or the person who starts a business, a ministry, a church a platform to collect tithes, offerings, or to be financially stable. You know a person is motivated by wrong motives because God is an afterthought. They sell you a dream of financial independence, wealth and prosperity for your comfort but they minimize that the purpose really should be to advance God's kingdom. Facebook is full of people who are social media famous. They built platforms and status with wrong motives. How do we know this is a false identity? It is simply one of the reasons why our prayers are not answered is that we have false motives. How many of us have had clients who go from one relationship to the next looking for love in all the wrong places?

I had a client who was a Christian but kept wanting to apply scripture to a relationship that was clearly unhealthy and not of God. He wanted God to bless his mess. The reason why God didn't answer the prayer was that it was clearly out of his will, the other reason why was because he was looking to man to fulfill a void that only God could fill. God is not going to give you something or someone to replace Him.

James 4:1-3 Living Bible (TLB)

1 What is causing the quarrels and fights among you? Isn't it because there is a whole army of evil desires within you?

2 You want what you don't have, so you kill to get it. You long for what others have, and can't afford it, so you start a fight to take it away from them. And yet the reason you don't have what you want is that you don't ask God for it.

3 And even when you do ask you don't get it because your whole aim is wrong—you want only what will give you pleasure.

Another symptom of a false identity is someone who constantly complains. A pet peeve of mine is when I have a client who wants to use their therapy sessions as complain session, they really don't want solutions they want someone to hear their complaint. Complaining is a symptom of ungratefulness, the learned helplessness, and the victim mentality. Complaining is a symptom that a person experiences intense fear and anxiety. The people of Israel were infamous for their complaints against God. Yet if you look at when they complained it was always a reaction to fear, an uncertain situation or a fearful situation where they couldn't see what was going to happen.

One Lord One Body Ministries, posted an interesting article where they chronicled how and when the people of Israel complained. The title is; How Israel Complaining 14 times mirrors your Christian Journey.

1 – The people complained to Moses that because of Him and His talk of a promise land, Pharaoh made things worse for them – Exodus 5:1-22.

2 – The people complained and said to Moses "let us alone" – Exodus 14:11-12

3 – The people complained about the bitter water – Exodus 15:22

4 – The people complained about being hungry; God gave them Manna – Exodus 16:1-4

5 – The people complained about being thirsty – Exodus 17:1-4 This is when your spiritual growth produces greater thirst.

6 – The people forsake the Lord. The Lord orders the Levites to kill 3000 people by the sword, because they worshipped the golden calf. – Exodus 32:28 .

7 – The "mixed multitude" of the people complained about food – Numbers 11

8 – Miriam and Aaron complain about Moses' leadership – The Lord curses Miriam with leprosy – Numbers 12:1-12

9 – The people complained about how difficult it looked to enter the land so they refused to enter the Promise Land. Numbers 14:1-10

10 – The people complained again and wanted to kill Moses – try to select another leader.

11 – The key leaders rebel against Moses – Numbers 16 –

12 – The people complained again and they accuse Moses of killing God's people – Numbers 16:41

13 – The people contended with Moses again because of no water – Moses gets angry Numbers 20:1-5

14 – The people complained against God and Moses – Numbers 21:4

How Israel Complaining 14 times mirrors your Christian Journey. (n.d) Retrieved from. https://onelordonebody.com/2014/02/27/how-israel-complaining-14-times-mirrors-your-christian-journey/. Retrieved on April 16, 2018.

I encourage you to read the article yourself. It is really an eye-opener. Joyce Meyers coined the term complain and remain. It means that when you keep complaining you remain. You can't complain yourself into a blessing. How do we know this is a false identity? Because of the examples are given. Also, if you look very carefully at each incident, God didn't respond very well to the people of Israel's complaints.

Numbers 11:1 Living Bible (TLB)

11 The people were soon complaining about all their misfortunes, and the Lord heard them. His anger flared out against them because of their complaints, so the fire of the Lord began destroying those at the far end of the camp.

Exodus 16:7 (TLB)

7-9 In the morning you will see more of his glory; for he has heard your complaints against him (for you aren't really complaining against us—who are we?)

When we complain God doesn't show us compassion, He takes it as if you are complaining against Him, even though if you look at the different examples in the article, the people never complained directly against God. They complained about Moses, their circumstances but they never said, "God you"

When we complain we really are not complaining about our situation we are really complaining against God because ultimately, we know that He is the only one that has the power to change it. Trust me I have been around this mountain many times on my journey. I could literally write a book about why you shouldn't complain. Before we move forward let's look at God's response to Job when he complained to God.

Job 40:1-14 Living Bible (TLB)

1 The Lord went on:

2 "Do you still want to argue with the Almighty? Or will you yield? Do you—God's critic—have the answers?"

3 Then Job replied to God:

4 "I am nothing—how could I ever find the answers? I lay my hand upon my mouth in silence.

5 I have said too much already."

6 Then the Lord spoke to Job again from the whirlwind:

7 "Stand up like a man and brace yourself for battle. Let me ask you a question, and give me the answer.

8 Are you going to discredit my justice and condemn me so that you can say you are right?

9 Are you as strong as God, and can you shout as loudly as he?

10 All right then, put on your robes of state, your majesty and splendor.

11 Give vent to your anger. Let it overflow against the proud.

12 Humiliate the haughty with a glance; tread down the wicked where they stand.

13 Knock them into the dust, stone-faced in death.

14 If you can do that, then I'll agree with you that your own strength can save you

It's got good, I encourage you to read Job 38, Job 39, Job 40, Job 41 it is good. You'll think twice about complaining. God was like, "you want to question my decision, okay Job."

Ultimately, we complain because we feel as though God is cheating us somehow. Job was a righteous man but a lot of traumatic and hurtful things happened to him. God still didn't respond to his complaints with compassion. You will also find this complaining identity among individuals who are secretly envious and bitter towards God. They secretly are angry for what has happened, why a loved one died, why they experienced the trauma they experienced. We are not here to judge them rather walk them through the healing process.

I could give you a full-on talk for hours about this particular false identity, but we must move forward. The only way to overcome this false identity is to be intentional about practicing gratefulness.

Psalm 107:1 Living Bible (TLB)

107 Say thank you to the Lord for being so good, for always being so loving and kind.

\Matthew 25:23 Living Bible (TLB)

23 "'Good work,' his master said. 'You are a good and faithful servant. You have been faithful over this small amount, so now I will give you much more.

Another word of faithful is grateful. If you thank God for what He has done and be grateful for it. Focus your mind on what you do have and not what you don't have it will change your mental disposition from depression to joy. Then God promises to give us more, the KJV version says if you are faithful over a few things He will make you ruler over many.

A ruler is a person exercising government or dominion. A ruler is also someone who makes you mean do something, to cause (something) to exist or come about; bring about. Faithfulness and gratefulness puts you in position to manifest the promises of God.

The next false identity is a spirit of entitlement. Feeling entitled means you feel you of have a right to have, do, or get something that you have not earned or worked for. The feeling or belief that you deserve to be given something. People that are entitled are very ungrateful. This is the person that thinks you must do something. We have already talked about this in detail, so I won't belabor the point. Entitled people want something they haven't worked for. Entitled people want positions but they don't have the character or integrity to keep them in the position. They want success with no effort.

These are people who want to shout about the promises of God but don't want to put in any effort. They want God to bless their finances but don't want to pay their tithes.

James 2:14 (NKJV)

14 What does it profit, my brethren, if someone says he has faith but does not have works? Can faith save him?

James 2:18-20 (NKJV)

18 But someone will say, "You have faith, and I have works." Show me your faith without your[a] works, and I will show you my faith by my[b] works.

19 You believe that there is one God. You do well. Even the demons believe—and tremble!

20 But do you want to know, O foolish man, that faith without works is dead?[c]

The next false identity is it's all about me mentality. It simply means our thoughts, ideas are focused on self. An extreme is when a person has narcissistic personalities

Narcissistic Personality Disorder (NPD) is grandiosity, a lack of empathy for other people, and a need for admiration. Individuals with NPD seek excessive admiration and attention in order to know that others think highly of them.

Job 28:14 (NKJV)

14 The deep says, 'It is not in me';

And the sea says, 'It is not with me.'

Sometimes we just have to focus our minds off of ourselves.

Another false identity is a rebellious person. These are people who don't want to believe what God says. They don't want to follow God's will. We can't think of God and embrace His identity if you don't believe or want to submit to His word.

1 Samuel 15:23 Living Bible (TLB)

23 For rebellion is as bad as the sin of witchcraft, and stubbornness is as bad as worshiping idols. And now because you have rejected the word of Jehovah, he has rejected you from being king.

Examples of this are individuals who want God's blessing but don't want to follow His way.

2 Timothy 3:5-7 (KJV)

5 Having a form of godliness, but denying the power thereof: from such turn away.

6 For of this sort are they which creep into houses, and lead captive silly women laden with sins, led away with divers lusts,

7 Ever learning, and never able to come to the knowledge of the truth.

Another false identity is a shame-based nature. You will find this in individuals who have experienced long-term sexual trauma over an extended period. Shame is the painful feeling arising from the consciousness of something dishonorable, improper, ridiculous, etc., done by oneself or another: to cause to feel shame; make ashamed: Shame, embarrassment, mortification, humiliation, chagrin designate different kinds or degrees of painful.

Shamed based nature (n.d)
http://www.dictionary.com/browse/shame. Retrieved on April 16, 2018.

You can feel shame so long it becomes a part of your personality and affects every area of life including relationships. You will also find excessive guilt and self-blame in survivors of sexual trauma.

Isaiah 50:7-9 (TLB)

7 Because the Lord God helps me, I will not be dismayed; therefore, I have set my face like flint to do his will, and I know that I will triumph.

8 He who gives me justice is near. Who will dare to fight against me now? Where are my enemies? Let them appear!

9 See, the Lord God is for me! Who shall declare me guilty? All my enemies shall be destroyed like old clothes eaten up by moths!

God doesn't accuse you. Satan does.

Revelation 12:10-11 Living Bible (TLB)

10 Then I heard a loud voice shouting across the heavens, "It has happened at last! God's salvation and the power and the rule, and the authority of his Christ are finally here; for the Accuser of our brothers has been thrown down from heaven onto earth—he accused them day and night before our God.

11 They defeated him by the blood of the Lamb and by their testimony; for they did not love their lives but laid them down for him.

If we submit to Jesus we win, Satan loses.

The final false identity we will discuss is the fear conscious. These are individuals who worry and are afraid so often they believe that fear is a part of their lives. You will find this in clients who say, "I am just a worrier, I have always been a worrier, everyone in my family is a worrier." A fear conscious means to simply live in fear and to constantly be worried about what could happen. I dedicate entire sessions and treatment plans solely for individuals who have a fear conscious. I encourage you to pick up my book; No Fear and the workbook, Fight Fear With Faith. How do we know this is a false identity?

2 Timothy 1:7 (KJV)

7 For God hath not given us the spirit of fear; but of power, and of love, and of a sound mind.

At times I dedicate sessions to looking at Psalms 91 and given therapeutic homework based upon Psalms 91.

Psalm 91 (TLB)

1 We live within the shadow of the Almighty, sheltered by the God who is above all gods.

2 This I declare, that he alone is my refuge, my place of safety; he is my God, and I am trusting him.

3 For he rescues you from every trap and protects you from the fatal plague.

4 He will shield you with his wings! They will shelter you. His faithful promises are your armor.

 5 Now you don't need to be afraid of the dark anymore, nor fear the dangers of the day;

 6 nor dread the plagues of darkness, nor disasters in the morning.[a]

7 Though a thousand fall at my side, though ten thousand are dying around me, the evil will not touch me.

8 I will see how the wicked are punished, but I will not share it.

9 For Jehovah is my refuge! I choose the God above all gods to shelter me.

10 How then can evil overtake me or any plague come near?

11 For he orders his angels to protect you wherever you go.

12 They will steady you with their hands to keep you from stumbling against the rocks on the trail.

13 You can safely meet a lion or step on poisonous snakes, yes, even trample them beneath your feet!

14 For the Lord says, "Because he loves me, I will rescue him; I will make him great because he trusts in my name.

15 When he calls on me, I will answer; I will be with him in trouble and rescue him and honor him.

16 I will satisfy him with a full life[b] and give him my salvation."

Most identity issues boil down to being insecurity. Insecurity is not confident or assured; uncertain and anxious.

All false identity means is having a false sense of self we help the client to align their beliefs about themselves, God and their world to the word of God.

They must agree to believe, trust and learn. So how does this play out in session?

Educate/teach

Identify

Clarify

Restructure

We start by educating the client about the different types of false identities. By the way, we went over many of the different types of false identities nonetheless there are many more.

We then help the client to identify what false identity they most relate to and why.

We help them to clarify what the truth is based on the word of God. We give them ways to restructure their thoughts by applying the word of God to their circumstance.

After we provide education to the client about the different false identities, we have them to identify which identities they relate to.

Identify	Clarify	Restructure
What false identity most relates to me? Why? *Example: "I most identify with the imposture syndrome because I just feel like not matter what I am not what people think and will eventually be found out."*	What does God have to say about me? *Genesis 1:27 (TLB)* *27 So God made man like his Maker.* *Like God did God make man;* *Man and mad3 did he make them.* *1 Peter 2:9 (KJV)* *9 But ye are a chosen generation, a royal priesthood, a holy nation, a peculiar people; that ye should shew forth the praises of him who hath called you out of*	What is the truth of the matter? *"I have been made to be like God, I am not an imposture."* *"I have been chosen by God."*

	darkness into his marvelous light;	

Imposture Syndrome "I don't belong here.	Deuteronomy 28:13' I John 1:9 Philippians 4:14
Victim Mentality "Why are people always using me?"	I Corinthians 5:33
Learned Helplessness "I can't do it."	Philippians 4:13
Orphan Spirit, "No one loves me."	John 3:16
Performance Driven, Approval Addiction	Romans 8:13
Wrong Motives	Acts 8:8-21
Complaining	Psalms 107:1 Matthew 25:23
Entitlement	James 2:14 II Corinthians 2:18-20
Rebellious	I Samuel 15:23
Insecure	2 Timothy 1:7
Shame/Guilt	Isaiah 50:7-9
Fear	Psalms 91 II Timothy 1:7

We don't want to focus on what we are not, rather what we are. Give the client scriptures to meditate on, the scriptures should be the promises of God that directly confront a false identity.

10 Scriptures About God's Promises

2 Peter 1:4

And because of his glory and excellence, he has given us great and precious promises. These are the promises that enable you to share his divine nature and escape the world's corruption caused by human desires.

Jeremiah 29:11

For I know the plans I have for you," says the Lord. "They are plans for good and not for disaster, to give you a future and a hope.

Matthew 11:28-29

"Come to me, all you who are weary and burdened, and I will give you rest. Take my yoke upon you and learn from me, for I am gentle and humble in heart, and you will find rest for your souls.

Isaiah 40:29-31

He gives power to the weak

and strength to the powerless.

Even youths will become weak and tired,

and young men will fall in exhaustion.

But those who trust in the Lord will find new strength.

They will soar high on wings like eagles.

They will run and not grow weary.

They will walk and not faint.

Philippians 4:19

And this same God who takes care of me will supply all your needs from his glorious riches, which have been given to us in Christ Jesus.

Romans 8:37-39

No, despite all these things, overwhelming victory is ours through Christ, who loved us. And I am convinced that nothing can ever separate us from God's love. Neither death nor life, neither angels nor demons, neither our fears for today nor our worries about tomorrow—not even the powers of hell can separate us from God's love. No power in the sky above or in the earth below—indeed, nothing in all creation will ever be able to separate us from the love of God that is revealed in Christ Jesus our Lord.

Proverbs 1:33

But all who listen to me will live in peace,

untroubled by fear of harm."

John 14:27

"I am leaving you with a gift—peace of mind and heart. And the peace I give is a gift the world cannot give. So don't be troubled or afraid.

Romans 10:9

If you confess with your mouth that Jesus is Lord and believe in your heart that God raised him from the dead, you will be saved.

Romans 6:23

For the wages of sin is death, but the free gift of God is eternal life through Christ Jesus our Lord.

Ultimately healing and transformation takes place when we believe who what God has declared over our lives.

Chapter 9

Unconscious Defense Mechanisms

2 Corinthians 10:5-7 (NKJV)

5 casting down arguments and every high thing that exalts itself against the knowledge of God, bringing every thought into captivity to the obedience of Christ, 6 and being ready to punish all disobedience when your obedience is fulfilled.

In the counseling sessions, you will be confronted with individual barriers and strongholds that if not dealt with the counselee can get stuck. Getting stuck is where the individual stops making progress within the counseling session, and in some cases begins to decompensate. We must explore the unconscious defense mechanisms. This is something you need to be particularly aware of when counseling someone who is in ministry. Unconscious defense mechanisms are not the same as a false identity. Unconscious defenses mechanisms are what you do as a result of a false identity. Unconscious defense mechanisms are unhealthy responses that we do in order to cope with difficult feelings and emotions. We call them unconscious because these maladaptive responses we use so much, we may not know that we are using an unconscious defense mechanism.

Conscious is what you are aware of the unconscious, is a response that you do that you are not aware of.

We must take time to consider some psychological terms that will be important to our journey as counselors and why some client's get stuck or don't return.

Terms we will discuss is masking personality, co-dependency, dysfunctional family patterns. Dysfunctional family roles, intergenerational family coping mechanisms, familiar spirits, reversal roles such as child-mothers, child fathers, emotional incest, unmet emotional needs. Some of you may be familiar with some of the terms that we have identified, now let's define them. I will give you the secular definition and the biblical definition.

First, let us define exactly what a defense mechanism it.

A defense mechanism is an unconscious psychological mechanism that reduces anxiety arising from unacceptable or potentially harmful stimuli.

Defense Mechanism.
https://en.wikipedia.org/wiki/Defence_mechanisms. Retrieved on March 30, 2017.

A defense mechanism is often unconscious mental process (such as repression) that makes possible compromise solutions to personal problems.

Defense Mechanisms.
https://www.merriamwebster.com/dictionary/defense%20mecha
nism. Retrieved March 20, 2017

So in layman's term, an unconscious defense mechanism is an invisible, unconscious term for an individual's attempt to avoid emotional pain by unconscious words, acts, deeds, or internal responses. Emphasis on the term unconscious. Unconscious means not knowing, unaware, not knowing or perceiving.

Have you ever been driving, and you got to your destination but didn't remember the drive? Maybe you have taken that same road so many times that your mind was elsewhere while you drove to your destination. I do not recommend this of course but am using this as an example. Have you ever known someone who was unconscious or in a coma? It is said that they can hear what is being said but have no ability to respond.

That mind is like a computer it remembers but sometimes with painful memories, it will hide things so deep you don't know that they are there, but they are very real. This will be present at times when dealing with trauma survivors, their minds will hide the memory of the trauma to the point where the counselee doesn't remember. Yet when assessing for post-traumatic stress disorder they meet all the criteria or have many of the long-term effects of the trauma that they don't remember.

Often a person may not be aware that they are using unconscious unhealthy defense mechanisms. Most of the unconscious defense mechanisms are unhealthy for us, we use them to get through what we are going through. The good news is God has a better way. Unconscious defense mechanisms become strongholds if we leave them unchecked.

Now about those terms let's go back and define them.

Masking personality-Masking is a process in which an individual changes or "masks" their natural personality to conform to social pressures, abuse, and/or harassment.

Masking Personality (n.d)
https://en.wikipedia.org/wiki/Masking_(personality)Retrieved on March 20, 2017

Examples of this can be found in teenagers that conform to social pressures, so they take on the personality of their peers. Say a young boy who is a straight-A student, but he doesn't want to be perceived as a nerd or he is teased by his peers, so he takes another persona to be excepted. Maybe his grades drop, maybe he starts acting as if he doesn't care.

I mentioned something about minsters earlier. You will find this evident if you are counseling someone who is in ministry. They may be not be fully honest about how they feel for fear of being misjudged. Often as Christians, we are taught that we are not supposed to be afraid, anxious or depressed. I agree that the Holy Spirit gives us peace and joy. Yet, we still struggle with these things in our humanity. Yes, God can and will deliver, but He won't deliver you from a problem that you won't acknowledge. This is very important counselors because you can't counsel someone who can't admit that they have a problem.

If there is no problem to confront with the word of God, then there is no resolution.

Often we are taught this name it and claim it mentality. That is if we name it the negative emotions and claim it then it becomes a part of us. Don't get me wrong there is some truth in that if you say, you are broke then you are broke. If you say you are going to lose your mind, then you will lose your mind. The key is in the purpose.

You and the counselee are not to claim something that is not there, you are to identify the problem. You are naming the problem, with the purpose of healing from it. You are identifying what the problem is so that you can know what actions to take.

Examples of this can be found in the word of God.

Luke 8:30 (NKJV)

30 Jesus asked him, saying, "What is your name?"

And he said, "Legion," because many demons had entered him.

Jesus was not claiming a demon's spirit, no He was identifying what was already there for real deliverance to take place within the person. So that is why Jesus asked the demon what his name was. He wasn't bringing the demon to the man he was simply using discernment to identify what was already there.

That is what Christian counselors do, we are not getting you to claim a spirit or a diagnosis, we are simply identifying what is already there so real deliverance can take place. What we didn't read in Luke was that after this Jesus cast out the demon called Legion. I encourage you to read further in your own time.

This is so important because the church culture as we know it there is a distrust of doctors, lawyers, and counselors. I have lost count as to how many times I have heard a pastor make a statement about doctors and counselors in rude demeaning ways.

Friends doctors, lawyers, psychiatrist, therapist are not our enemy. They are not the church's enemy. If that was the case, then why was Luke a physician allowed to write a testament in the bible? Why does Proverbs talk multiple times about counselors? Why are lawyers represented in the bible as well?

As counselors you will be confronted with church culture in the counselees you see, it is okay to be led by the Holy Spirit to confront these strongholds because if a person doesn't get over their hiccup with help agents it can delay and, in some cases, stop the healing process. There is so much more that I can say about this topic, but I must me move on. Maybe one day in another book I will address this further.

I know I have repeatedly said this but before we move to the next defense mechanism I must say this again, you cannot get healed or delivered from what you don't acknowledge.

The next defense mechanism is codependency. Co-dependency is excessive emotional or psychological reliance on a partner, typically a partner who requires support due to an illness or addiction. In other words, codependence is being so emotionally, mentally and spiritually intertwined with another human being so that the individual cannot make decisions without the person or their emotional state is interwoven in an unhealthy way to another person.

According to WebMD. Co-dependency is;

Being unable to find satisfaction in your life outside of a specific person.

Recognizing unhealthy behaviors in your partner but staying.

Giving support to your partner at the cost of your own mental, emotional, and physical health.

Codependent Relationships (n.d) http://www.webmd.com/sex-relationships/features/signs-of-a-codependent-relationship#1. Retrieved on March 20, 2017

Remember I said that the world takes biblical principles gives it a different name. In Christendom, we refer to codependency as a soul tie. A soul tie is an unhealthy, spiritual connection to the soul of another person.

Prophet Kris Vallotton gives us 7 characteristics of someone that is in a soul tie.

7 SIGNS THAT YOU HAVE AN UNHEALTHY SOUL TIE:

1. You are in a physically, and/or emotionally, and/or spiritually abusive relationship, but you "feel" so attached to them that you refuse to cut off the connection and set boundaries with them.

2. You have left a relationship (maybe long ago), but you think about the other person obsessively (you can't get them out of your mind).

3. Whenever you do anything – make a decision, have a conversation with someone etc., you "feel" like this person is with you or watching you.

4. When you have sex with someone else (hopefully your husband or wife), you can hardly keep yourself from visualizing the person you have a soul tie with.

5. You take on the negative traits of the person that your soul is tied to and carry their offenses whether or not you actually agree with them.

6. You defend your right to stay in a relationship with the person that your soul is tied to, even though it is negatively effecting or even destroying the important relationships in your life (husband, wife, kids, leaders, etc.)

7. You have simultaneous experiences and/or "moods" as the person your soul is tied to. This can even include sickness, accidents, addictions etc.1 Corinthians 6:15 – Do you not know that the one who joins himself to a prostitute is one body with her? For He says, "THE TWO SHALL BECOME ONE FLESH."

Vallotton, Kris (n.d) 7 Signs Of Unhealthy Soul Tie. Retrieved from http://krisvallotton.com/7-signs-of-an-unhealthy-soul-tie/. Retrieved on March 20, 2017.

Again, we didn't go into more specifics about codependency, but the same characteristics of codependency are the exact same as soul ties. In fact, we could take out the word soul tie, and put in co-dependency and get the same definition and long term effects.

This is so important to us as Christian counselors because the world has a basic knowledge of treatment for co-dependency but we in Christ have the answer.

Co-dependency really is a spiritual condition it must be addressed from the spirit realm. The secular counseling community cannot address it as a spiritual issue because they are not spiritual. Remember in Christ we have the answers to what the world needs.

This is also where the counselor must be well versed in deliverance ministry because at some point the soul tie when a person stays in this relationship too long, will take on demonic entities. Again, the secular counseling world has no idea how to combat demonic warfare. If the therapist is not trained, or well versed in deliverance ministry as appropriate refer them to a session with a deliverance minister.

The Christian counselor must understand how to address and do spiritual surgery on the counselee.

Transgenerational trauma that is transferred from the first generation of trauma survivors to the second and further generations of offspring of the survivors via complex post-traumatic stress disorder mechanisms.

In economics, the cycle of poverty is the "set of factors or events by which poverty, once started, is likely to continue unless there is outside intervention".[1]

The cycle of poverty has been defined as a phenomenon where poor families become impoverished for at least three generations, i.e. for enough time that the family includes no surviving ancestors who possess and can transmit the intellectual, social, and cultural capital necessary to stay out of or change their impoverished condition. In calculations of expected generation length and ancestor lifespan, the lower median age of parents in these families is offset by the shorter lifespans in many of these groups.

The cycle of Poverty (n.d) https://en.wikipedia.org/wiki/Cycle_of_poverty. Retrieved on March 17, 2018.

Scripture defined these terms early as generational curses, the reference to the scripture is found in that states that God would release a curse to the third and fourth Deuteronomy 5.

Deuteronomy 5:10

…… I will bring the curse of a father's sins upon even the third and fourth generation of the children of those who hate me;…..

It is by no accident that the cycles are about three generations to the cycle of poverty, but scripture says that God would release a curse to the third generation.

On to the next:

Parentification is the process of role reversal whereby a child is obliged to act as a parent to their own parent. In extreme cases, the child is used to fill the void of the alienating parent's emotional life.[1]

Two distinct modes of parentification have been identified technically: instrumental parentification and emotional parentification. Instrumental parentification involves the child completing physical tasks for the family, such as looking after a sick relative, paying bills, or providing assistance to younger siblings that would normally be provided by a parent. Emotional parentification occurs when a child or adolescent must take on the role of a confidant or mediator for (or between) parents or family members.[2]

Some call this parentified child syndrome, this is when the child takes on the role of the parent. They either become the mother or father to their parent. Children can take on the responsibility of caring for their parents as if they were the parent. Or they take on the responsibility of being a parent to their younger siblings.

Parentification (n.d)
https://en.wikipedia.org/wiki/Parentification. Retrieved on March 20, 2017.

I first saw this with my own eyes almost 15 years ago. I went to Zimbabwe and saw children ran homes. Either the parent was sick and unable to care for the child, or the parents had died from AIDS and the oldest child was found to be taking care of their younger siblings.

In America, we see more of this when parents are addicted to drugs and alcohol. The child takes on the responsibility of raising the younger siblings or raising parents.

Even when there is no substance abuse, we typically see the child having to raise their parents, as the parent takes on the child role. I am not referring to the end of life care that we see when the parents become elderly and their child takes on the role of caring for the parent.

As counselors, you will see this manifest in relationships. The counselee may not see this as a problem until they get into serious relationships. T.D Jakes came out with a movie some years ago entitled: Jumping The Broom. In the movie, the main character is getting married, but his mother tries to sabotage the relationship because she feels as though she may lose a son. The story is fictional, but the scenarios are not all fictional.

We see this type in single-parent homes. This is where the son was raised by his mother. Somewhere along the way, the son takes on the role of the husband to his mother, minus the sexual intimacy of course. Other than that, every other role is the same.

This becomes a problem because eventually, the man wants to get married and have a family of his own. He then meets a woman who he identifies he wants to marry. In some cases, if the issue is not dealt with it becomes a bigger issue in their marriage. The issue is that the mother doesn't see the wife or fiancé as her gaining a daughter, she sees the woman as competition. The reason why she sees the woman as competition is because the son has taken on the emotional role, and in some cases the burden of the husband. Mom doesn't have a man; because her son is her man. I call this emotional incest. We know what incest is but for the sake of the text let's go there.

Incest is sexual relations between people classed as being too closely related to marry each other. Incest is the crime of having sexual intercourse with a parent, child, sibling, or grandchild. Notice it says this is a crime. In the kingdom of God emotional incest is just as much a crime as physical incest. Therefore the bible says when a man is grown and married he has to leave and cleave.

Emotional incest, also known as covert incest, is a dynamic that occurs in parenting where the parent seeks emotional support through their child that should be sought through an adult relationship. Although the effects of emotional incest can be similar to those resulting from physical incest, the term does not encompass sexual abuse.

Emotional Covert Incest When Parents Make Their Kids, Their Partner (n.d) https://www.goodtherapy.org/blog/emotional-covert-incest-when-parents-make-their-kids-partners-0914165. Retrieved on March 20, 2017

Covert incest, also known as emotional incest, is a style of parenting in which a parent looks to their child for the emotional support that would be normally provided by another adult.[1] The effects of covert incest on children when they become adults are thought to mimic actual incest, although to a lesser degree.

Covert incest is described as occurring when a parent is unable or unwilling to maintain a relationship with another adult and forces the emotional role of a spouse onto their child instead.[8] The child's needs are ignored and instead, the relationship exists solely to meet the needs of the parent[1][3] and the adult may not be aware of the issues created by their actions.[11

Covert Incest (n.d) Retrieved from https://en.wikipedia.org/wiki/Covert_incest. Retrieved on April 20, 2017

Scripture is clear about the stance of marital relationships.

Genesis 2:24 (KJV)

24 Therefore shall a man leave his father and his mother, and shall cleave unto his wife: and they shall be one flesh.

Leave and cleave is not just a physical state of being, but a mental and emotional state.

I am going to ask you a silly question that I am sure you know the answer to, but I need you to think about it. What do you call it when a man starts engaging in a relationship with another woman who is not his wife?

Adultery is voluntary sexual intercourse between a married person and a person who is not his or her spouse.

When an individual continues in an emotional incestual relationship with someone who is not their spouse in Christendom we consider this emotional adultery. It doesn't matter who it is. That would include with a biological parent.

An emotional affair (emotional adultery) can be defined as: "A relationship between a person and someone other than (their) spouse (or lover) that affects the level of intimacy, emotional distance and overall dynamic balance in the marriage. The role of an affair is to create emotional distance in the marriage."

Emotional Affair (n.d) Retrieved from, https://en.wikipedia.org/wiki/Emotional_affair. Retrieved on March 20, 2017

The term often describes a bond between two people that mimics the closeness and emotional intimacy of a romantic relationship while never being physically consummated.

An emotional affair is sometimes referred to as an affair of the heart. An emotional affair may emerge from a friendship, and progress toward greater levels of personal intimacy and attachment. What distinguishes an emotional affair from a friendship is the assumption of emotional roles between the two participants that mimic of those of an actual relationship - with regards to confiding personal information and turning to the other person during moments of vulnerability or need.

Emotional Affair (n.d) Retrieved from, https://en.wikipedia.org/wiki/Emotional_affair. Retrieved on March 20, 2017

As counselors, we must understand these concepts. I know I may have offended some of you yet if we want people to come to full deliverance we can't be afraid to confront them with the truth. A wife and the mother don't have the same platform, they should not hold the exact same emotional space in a man's heart. A man shouldn't put his wife and his mother at the same place in his life. According to scripture a man must leave where he was raised and be one with his wife. It doesn't say be one with his mother.

These breaches of boundaries create emotional distance between the husband and wife, and if unchecked can lead to divorce. I highlighted the son-mother role because that is what we tend to see more often, but you can see this in daughter-father roles. Again we tend to see it more in son mother roles because there is a long-standing epidemic in our world today of women raising boys on their own. I am not suggesting that all single parents are like this, but it something that you will see in counseling sessions, particularly for couples who come in for Christian marriage counselor.

Relationships require healthy boundaries. A boundary is not the same as a wall. No one is asking a counselee to disown their parents, or the mother, we are teaching them the importance of boundaries. Boundaries are just that boundaries, unofficial and official rules about what should not be done, limits that define acceptable behavior.

Notice also the scripture say the husband is the head of his wife, it never said he was the head of his mother.

Ephesians 5:23 (KJV)

23 For the husband is the head of the wife, even as Christ is the head of the church: and he is the saviour of the body.

Another concept we need to talk about is unmet emotional needs. When we have unmet emotional needs we tend to revert back to unconscious defense mechanisms.

Just like we have physical needs for our wellbeing such as clothes, food, shelter. We have emotional needs.

The emotional need is a psychological or mental requirement of intrapsychic origin that usually centers on such basic feelings as love, fear, anger, sorrow, anxiety, frustration, and depression and involves the understanding, empathy, and support of one person for another.

Medical dictionary.thefreedictionary.com/emotional need

We learned concepts in graduate school about Maslow hierarchy of needs.

Maslow Hierarchy of Needs (n.d) Retrieved from. https://www.google.com/imgres?imgurl=https://www.simplypsychology.org/maslow.jpg&imgrefurl. Retrieved on March 20, 2017

Notice in the diagram that basic needs were at the bottom, but as we go up the emotional needs are at the top. It tells us that as human beings we place a great deal of emphasis on emotional needs and when they are not met there are deficits in our lives.

It is my belief that what we are longing for really is for the Father. We were created to be fulfilled and to worship God. When we don't know Him or our relationship with Him is not there as it should be what we created is an emotional, mental and spiritual deficit.

So how does what we talked about play out as an unconscious defense mechanism? These defense mechanisms are what you the counselor will be confronted with in session.

Denial a person may be the super spiritual saint who denies they have a problem while their life is falling apart.

Regression is when an individual reverts to an earlier stage we discussed this in detail about child parents and emotional incest.

Acting out, in children or fits of rage in adults.

Dissociation is when a person loses track of time or places. They don't remember painful events this is present when counseling's those who have experienced severe sexual abuse and trauma.

Compartmentalization- when a person has two set of values. Examples being the pastor who preaches against sin in the church, but then turns around and cheats on his wife.

Projection-when an individual has unpleasant thoughts about themselves but instead of acknowledging it they project or displaces their feelings about themselves onto another.

Reaction Formation-converting unwanted thoughts into the opposite action. Examples being the woman who is so angry at how she is treated by her mother, she responds by being overly kind, allow herself to be manipulated and never speak up.

Repression-blocking unacceptable thoughts, feelings, and impulses.

Displacement-similar to the projection, however, the person redirects the thoughts, feelings, and impulses of one person or object and takes it out on another. Examples being the man who is angry about how he is treated at work then goes home and takes it out on his wife and kids by beating them.

Intellectualization-you try to explain away with facts and figures. You find this within Christendom when a leader is caught in sin, instead of humility admitting their wrong, they instead use scripture to justify their actions.

Rationalization is making light of something. Examples being the person found caught in sin, and they make a statement like, "well everybody does it, or no man can judge me but God."

Undoing- trying to take back an unconscious behavior. In Christendom, this is displayed with religious spirits who try to earn their way to heaven or seek their works as their salvation.

Procrastination is the action of delaying or postponing something. Saying, "I do it tomorrow and tomorrow never comes."

Proverbs 6:6-8 (KJV)

6 Go to the ant, thou sluggard; consider her ways, and be wise:

7 Which having no guide, overseer, or ruler,

8 Provideth her meat in the summer, and gathereth her food in the harvest.

Proverbs 6:4 (NIV)

4 Allow no sleep to your eyes,

   no slumber to your eyelids.

Passiveness-accepting or allowing what happens or what others do, without active response or resistance. Passiveness is really a demonic spirit, found in King Ahab that lives on today. See I Kings 17 and read through for scriptural references

Aggressiveness-ready or likely to attack or confront; characterized. This presents itself when a person is angry, and masking hurt feelings. This person presents as very defensive and hard to confront even if it is done with great respect.

So how does the Christian counselor address such a person? For these responses, there is not a direct answer. Again, you have to use the gifts of the spirit. However, Timothy 4 gives us some direction.

Timothy 4:2 (NKJV)

2 Preach the word! Be ready in season and out of season. Convince, rebuke, exhort, with all longsuffering and teaching.

2 Timothy 4:2 (KJV)

2 Preach the word; be instant in season, out of season; reprove, rebuke, exhort with all long suffering and doctrine.

There are other defense mechanisms that we won't have time to address. Yet, when getting resistance from a counselee, you must use the Word, the Word, the Word of God. You must be led by the Holy Spirit. He is the answer. It is only the word of God that can pierce hardened hearts.

Hebrews 4:12 (KJV)

12 For the word of God is quick, and powerful, and sharper than any two edged sword, piercing even to the dividing asunder of soul and spirit, and of the joints and marrow, and is a discerner of the thoughts and intents of the heart.

The word of God pierces through all resistance.

Allow the Holy Spirit to take over, point out to the counselee where they are using a defense mechanism and confront them with the word. Pray for them, continue to move forward with the counseling session.

Chapter 10

Mindfulness For Christians

1 Corinthians 14:15 (KJV)

15 What is it then? I will pray with the spirit, and I will pray with the understanding also: I will sing with the spirit, and I will sing with the understanding also.

Mindfulness is something you will hear about in counseling communities. Many Christians get weirded out by the word mindfulness because of how we perceive it. Remember the diagram I showed you earlier with the lady sitting on the floor with her hands in the air and her knees folded. Yet there are ways that we can practice mindfulness without compromising our faith. The basic definition of mindfulness is simply being present and having a strategy for how you will regulate your emotions.

What happens when you are on the verge of a panic attack? What do you do when worry wants to creep in and consume you? How do you manage your emotions when they want to go out of whack? Life will throw you some boulders that you were not anticipating. You must know to keep calm and face it head-on.

This last chapter will give you basic strategies to teach your clients how to not allow their emotions to rule. Some of the things we have already gone over in previous chapters.

You don't wait until you are on the verge of a break down before you have a strategy you have a strategy in advance. This will be very different from what you learn in traditional mental health circles. As stated we are learning to do things through Christ.

The reason why you shouldn't practice traditional mindful methods is most if not all of them start in religious roots that are contrary to the word of God. Many of these methods teach us to worship false idols, false religions and in many cases are dedicated to demons of darkness. Anything rooted in new age methods, which most traditional mindfulness exercises are is not something we should be practicing.

We don't want to embrace new age, we want to embrace what the word of God has to say. Before we go into what we should be doing as Christian's let us consider what we shouldn't be doing. It is important to note that just because something looks helpful and appears helpful doesn't mean it is.

In an article by Charisma Magazine, they break down the reason why Christian shouldn't do yoga and other new age methodology.

6 Reasons This Popular Meditation Trend Is Dangerous for Christians. By Jukic Rosilind

We live in a very stressed-out culture that is constantly looking for ways to unwind and destress. Just about any doctor or health expert will tell you to do one thing: meditate.

By meditate they mean an Eastern form of meditation: Zen meditation, transcendental meditation, yoga, Chinese or Hindu meditation, guided meditation, all of which have their origins in new age and Eastern religions.

*The meditation God was talking about in Joshua 1:8 differs greatly from Eastern meditation. In fact, I'll go so far as to say that participating in **any form of meditation, apart from biblical meditation, is opening the door wide to the enemy**.*

When the Lord your God shall cut off the nations from before you, where you go to possess them, and you dispossess them, and dwell in their land, take heed to yourself so that you are not ensnared by following them, after they have been destroyed before you, and that you not inquire after their gods, saying, "How did these nations serve their gods? Even so I will do likewise." You shall not do so to the Lord your God, for every abomination to the Lord, which He hates, they have done to their gods. They have even burned their sons and their daughters in the fire to their gods.

Whatever I command you, be careful to do it. You shall not add to it or take away from it (Deut. 12:29-32).

Throughout the Bible He calls Himself jealous.

He has commanded us to keep our worship pure and undefiled by the worship of other gods. You may argue, "But I'm not using these other forms of meditation for worship." However, as Christians whatever we do in our life should be to glorify God, and if anything, we're doing does not glorify God—but, in fact, is used to glorify another god—we should immediately reject it and eliminate it from our lives!

This includes yoga, which many Christians engage in as a stress-relieving form of exercise. When you examine its origins and meaning, you can easily see why yoga has no place in the life of the believer.

However, like any other Christian discipline, biblical meditation should be part of our daily practice: speaking the Word, muttering it to ourselves, mulling over it, and imagining how our lives should fit in its context.

This takes the Word to a much deeper level than reading, studying, praying and even memorizing, as we contemplate deeply what each passage actually means for us personally and speaking it over and over to ourselves.

How does Eastern meditation differ from biblical meditation?

1. Eastern meditation empties the mind. Biblical meditation fills the mind and spirit with God's Word. Emptying our mind is actually a very dangerous thing because it gives the enemy room to fill it with his deception. However the Hebrew word for meditation actually means to speak or mutter, a practice that actually does the opposite of Eastern meditation. It fills our mind with God's Word and builds our spirit.

2. Eastern meditation focuses on self: centering yourself, your inner self, self-actualization, your breathing, physical feelings and emotions. The enemy will do anything to get us to stop focusing on Christ. Furthermore, his ultimate deception is pride or elevation of self. Biblical meditation takes our focus off of ourselves and places our focus on Jesus Christ.

3. Eastern meditation seeks to relieve stress. The problem with our culture isn't stress. Stress is only a symptom of a deeper problem: pride. Worry, fear, perfectionism ... these all have their root in pride and all result in stress. But God wants us to daily walk in faith that brings us peace no matter our circumstance. Jesus said, "Peace I leave with you. My peace I give to you; not as the world gives do I give to you. Let not your heart be troubled, neither let it be afraid" (John 14:27).

Christians absolutely shouldn't turn to anything other than Jesus Christ for the peace that will help to ease whatever it is that has brought stress on in their lives!

4. Eastern meditation focuses on man being in control. Eastern meditation practices rely on self as the agent to bring peace, tranquility and oneness with deity—the original lie: "You can become like God." Biblical meditation reminds us God is almighty and when He is in control we can be at complete peace knowing that His purposes will prevail. Eastern meditation dethrones God and puts fallen man in His place.

5. Eastern meditation is only escapism. By seeking higher levels of consciousness or altered states of consciousness you can escape your stress and enter new realms of oneness with deity. But the fact remains that once we have returned to our usual state of consciousness whatever it was that brought on the stress is still there. Biblical meditation doesn't give us an escape from reality, it gives us supernatural strength through the Holy Spirit to walk through the "fire and flood" at peace, knowing that God is in control of every situation. We don't need to escape our troubles; by faith we walk through them, counting it all joy, knowing that the testing of your faith produces patience.

6. Eastern meditation manipulates circumstances to bring peace. By using atmosphere, objects, silence, breathing techniques and more, people are able to enter a meditative state. It's a manipulation of circumstances and atmosphere. However, the child of God can meditate on God's Word whenever, wherever, no matter the situation or circumstance because we have direct access to the throne of God. Indeed, we are the temple of God and His Holy Spirit dwells within us. We never need to manipulate any situation to experience peace; we simply recall the precious promises of the Word of God and place our faith and trust in Him!

Rosilind, Jukic. (2016, July 18) 6 Reasons This Popular Meditation Trend Is Dangerous for Christians. Retrieved from, https://www.charismanews.com/opinion/58612-6-reasons-this-popular-meditation-trend-is-dangerous-for-christians on April 16, 2018.

I encourage you to read the authors article in its entirety the author did a wonderful job of explaining why we as Christians shouldn't practice yoga. Also, check out her website and support the other resources that she offers as alternatives to yoga. http://www.rosilindjukic.com/

The point is when we say practice mindfulness I am not referring to using worldly or secular methods, attempting to put a Jesus stamp on it and calling it a Christian method. As the author stated and I agree these new age methodologies are really the doctrine of demons that are meant to introduce us to the demonic world and cause us to submit to alternative idolatry and false worship.

So, what should you do?

We have already talked about meditating on the word of God extensively, so I won't belabor the point. Remember faith comes by hearing, and hearing and hearing the word of God. The more word you put in, the word will regulate you put you in a place of balance and help you to know what to do when you don't know. Yet let's go back to the scripture we read at the beginning of the chapter.

1 Corinthians 14:15 (KJV)

15 What is it then? I will pray with the spirit, and I will pray with the understanding also: I will sing with the spirit, and I will sing with the understanding also.

This scripture is the profound and meaningful scripture that you will need to implement to implement Christian mindfulness.

It first tells us to pray. I know you know what prayer is but there is nothing that will regulate your emotions like prayer. Look what the scripture says about the benefits of prayer.

After you pray the peace will come. Repeat it with me "after you pray the peace will come."

Philippians 4:4-7 (KJV)

4 Rejoice in the Lord always: and again I say, Rejoice.

5 Let your moderation be known unto all men. The Lord is at hand.

6 Be careful for nothing; but in every thing by prayer and supplication with thanksgiving let your requests be made known unto God.

7 And the peace of God, which passeth all understanding, shall keep your hearts and minds through Christ Jesus.

Where does anxiety, depression uncertainty come? In your heart and in your mind. Repeat it with me a third time, "after prayer comes peace." Look at the formulation for scriptural meditation and practicing Christian mindfulness. I don't want you to miss it. It says you start with rejoicing, moderation which means gentleness or balance, then pray, after that the peace will come.

Again, you start every pray with rejoicing. Don't start praying with complaints, but with joy. Then have a more balanced view of your circumstance, how do we express joy? Through kind words, gratefulness, singing, music.

Psalm 100:4 (NKJV)

4 Enter into His gates with thanksgiving,

And into His courts with praise.

Be thankful to Him, and bless His name.

What happens after you rejoice, the atmosphere begins to shift. You start changing your mind about what you were upset about. You begin to set the atmosphere for His presence to come. If you are offended by any person forgive. Be careful with nothing means don't take anything lightly. Then it says go into prayer. After that, the peace of God will come.

We must spend time with God and He will guard our hearts, and usher us into peace. So we practice mindful or mood regulation by filling our hearts up with prayer. It seems so simple but many people have a hard time praying. If you think about all our life responsibilities, work etc prayer at times can be the last on our list.

I have found in my life that a lot of the stress and worry I faced that day could have been avoided if I simply prayed. Always have a morning ritual where you spend time in the word of God and in prayer. You don't have to spend hours in prayer, but you don't want to miss it. If others have time to go to yoga, meditate in a secular sense trust me you have time to pray. Notice the scripture said that "I will pray with the spirit, I will sing with the spirit." We must invite the Holy Spirit into our prayer. There is nothing like regulating your mind like the Holy Spirit.

One of my clients taught me this, she said she gets up in the morning and turns on worship music. Worship music or worship sets the atmosphere for the peace of God to begin to rest. After she plays a song or two, she begins to write her prayer out or she just prays. You will literally feel the atmosphere of peace begin to shift and heaven rest, where the atmosphere has been set. These folks are turning to new age methods for peace but there is no peace like the Holy Spirit. Worship also helps to set your mind on Jesus.

The other thing that is probably the most important thing is you must pray in the spirit. Not just with the spirit but in the spirit. There is a difference.

Romans 8:25-27 (NKJV)

25 But if we hope for what we do not see, we eagerly wait for it with perseverance.

26 Likewise the Spirit also helps in our weaknesses. For we do not know what we should pray for as we ought, but the Spirit Himself makes intercession for us[a] with groanings which cannot be uttered.

27 Now He who searches the hearts knows what the mind of the Spirit is, because He makes intercession for the saints according to the will of God.

I know some of you reading this don't believe it speaking in tongues or you believe that speaking in tongues is not for you. Yet the truth is there are times when anxiety wants to consume us and we don't know what to pray. There are times when devastation wants to grip us we don't have words. There are times when we just need this supernatural power of God to shift us to divine boldness. There is no other force that will get us to the place, quickly and meticulously like the Holy Spirit and speak in your heavenly language. If you don't know about speaking in tongues just pray and ask God for the gift, your mind will not stay bound when you speak through the intercessory which is the Holy Spirit in His language.

Kenneth Copeland Ministries gives us great insight into the benefits of speaking in tongues;

5 Benefits of Praying in Tongues By Kenneth Copeland

When you are baptized in the Holy Spirit, you receive a gift from God—the gift of speaking (or praying) in tongues. It is a powerful gift that every believer should desire. In fact, here are five benefits to praying in tongues:

Praying in Tongues Allows You to Speak Directly to God

"For if you have the ability to speak in tongues, you will be talking only to God, since people won't be able to understand you. You will be speaking by the power of the Spirit, but it will all be mysterious." –1 Corinthians 14:2

When you pray in tongues, you are praying God's will, directly to Him. It allows your mind to get out of the way so your spirit can commune with the Father.

Praying in Tongues Keeps You in Tune With the Holy Spirit

"And everyone present was filled with the Holy Spirit and began speaking in other languages, as the Holy Spirit gave them this ability." –Acts 2:4

Tongues is a gift from God. It allows you to pray the will of God by the empowering of the Holy Spirit. When you pray in tongues, you are yielding to the Holy Spirit who dwells in you. Then you are allowing that same Spirit to pray through you, so you are in tune with Him.

Praying in Tongues Strengthens Your Spirit

"A person who speaks in tongues is strengthened personally, but one who speaks a word of prophecy strengthens the entire church." –1 Corinthians 14:4

Praying in tongues builds you up spiritually and helps you to live a Spirit-led life.

Praying in Tongues Allows You to Pray Even When You Don't Know What to Pray

"And the Holy Spirit helps us in our weakness. For example, we don't know what God wants us to pray for. But the Holy Spirit prays for us with groanings that cannot be expressed in words." –Romans 8:26

Even when you don't know how or what to pray, you can still pray…in tongues. You can trust your spirit to pray the perfect will of God, regardless of the situation.

Praying in Tongues Is a Weapon Against the Work of the Enemy

"And then he told them, 'Go into all the world and preach the Good News to everyone. Anyone who believes and is baptized will be saved.… These miraculous signs will accompany those who believe: They will cast out demons in my name, and they will speak in new languages.… They will be able to place their hands on the sick, and they will be healed.'" – Mark 16:15-18

Jesus proclaimed several things that would happen to those who followed Him and continued His work. Speaking in tongues is one of those gifts, and it allows Jesus' followers to stand against the work of the enemy.

Praying in tongues is a gift that's available to every believer. It allows you to pray God's will to Him. It keeps you in tune with the Holy Spirit and strengthens your spirit as you stand against the work of the devil. Don't discount this powerful gift from God. Desire it. Embrace it and relish the strength it adds to your spiritual life.

Copeland, Kenneth (n.d) 5 Benefits of Speaking In Tongues Retrieved from; http://www.kcm.org/real-help/prayer/apply/5-benefits-praying-tongues. Retrieved on April 16, 2018.

Other ways to practice emotion regulation is to play worship music. Sing songs unto the Lord. Always, always, always have your time with God.

Others ways to practice mindfulness is to be mindful what you allow in your spirit. When I was a little girl we would sing a song that went, "be careful little eyes what you see, be careful little eyes what you see, because the father up above is looking down below be careful little eyes what you see." It would go on with be careful what you hear etc.

The point is we were taught to be careful and not allow certain things into our spirits. This is a profound truth. You can't listen to dirt all day long and expect to stay clean. I almost never watch the news, because it triggers anxiety for me. I don't watch CSI, reality television, gossip shows, because that will trigger me. Some of the things we listen and watch are laced with the demonic. A Christian should never read or watch Harry Potter books. If you watch television shows like the Walking Dead you are bound for trouble. You can't get free from one thing, then turn around and watch that same thing on television or in music. I don't understand Christians who listen to sexually explicit R & B music and then wonder why they have a hard time maintaining sexual purity. What you put in, will come out. Again practicing mindfulness in this sense means guarding your heart, mind, and spirit. If a client is struggling with anxiety triggers we have to ask what happened? Did they allow something in their spirit that didn't belong there? I had clients who struggled with anxiety, but then watched the news all day long and then wondered why they were fearful about the future. You get what you put in.

Proverbs 4:23 (KJV)

23 Keep (Guard) thy heart with all diligence; for out of it are the issues of life

There is so much more that I could say but our time is just about at the end. You are probably thinking how does this relate to helping our client's do CCBT, it is simple we model behavior, we teach them how to study, how to meditate on scripture. We can't teach them how to speak in tongues only the Holy Spirit can do that, but we can teach them the benefits of it when they are open. Emphasis on when they are open. Warning don't weird them out.

How do you know they are ready? You start in small steps, by introducing them to a relationship with the Holy Spirit piece by piece bit by bit. You may want to pick up Benny Hinn's book; Good Morning Holy Spirit.

This phase of CCBT the more we practice it in our lives it will translate to our client's. My office has a peaceful atmosphere, so it helps for the presence of God to manifest. They ask about this peace and I tell them where it came from, it didn't' come from me, it comes from God. Funny story I had a client who complained that he hadn't slept in days. He gets into my office and while we are talking he couldn't keep his eyes open. To the average person, you may think I am such a bore that client's fall asleep in my office, at least the thought crossed my mind. Then he says, "I am so sorry I just haven't slept but it is so peaceful in here."

You know a person's anxiety and fear is decreasing when they are able to rest. Of course, I don't advocate them sleeping in my office LOL. (laugh out loud) The point is the atmosphere of peace was so full it calmed his fear. I have had client's say they didn't want to leave my office because it was so peaceful.

Is your office a place where the Holy Spirit can rest in? Did you set the atmosphere before they came? Play your worship music before the client gets there. Funny story I had a client arrive at my office and I didn't know she was there. I was the only one the office that day, so I am there singing and inviting the Holy Spirit in, and walks in and say, "you have a beautiful voice." Okay, it was not a joke, but the point is I was going into worship before she came. I have prayed Holy Spirit I welcome you into this place, have your way.

Therapist play music softly in their office all the time, but most of it is regular meditation music, not worship music. If secular therapist know how to set atmospheres so can we. I love to play my Hillsong, Bethel Music in between sessions. I want my office to be a space where not only the client feels welcome but the Holy Spirit fill welcome.

Other final things we can do is teach the client about confession. There is power in the confession.

Job 22:28 (KJV)

28 Thou shalt also decree a thing, and it shall be established unto thee: and the light shall shine upon thy ways.

Psalm 2:7 (KJV)

7 I will declare the decree: the Lord hath said unto me, Thou art my Son; this day have I begotten thee.

Declare means to proclaim with authority and confidence. Decree means to establish. Decree also means an official order issued by a legal authority.

How many of us have declared something negative? "I am sick, I am broke, I am poor." We talked about this in the identifying false identity chapter. Believe it or not, most people know how to declare something negative, they have not been taught the declaration of something positive.

I tell my client's when fear starts to talk to you talk back to fear. "Fear you are not going to get me today, fear I am not having it." This is different than affirmations. Affirmations mean to provide emotional support by speaking.

Declaring and decreeing has nothing to do with your emotions. When you declare and decree you proclaim the word of God. Remember we talked about the power of the word of God.

Elizabeth Dixon wrote an article in Charisma Today that answered the question, Are You Decreeing and Declaring in Your Prayers?

In the article, she is quoted saying,

The spiritual ramifications are stunning. We see here that when we decree, we:

1. speak God's blessings upon our lives,

2. institute the very will and purposes of God,

3. separate and destroy the plans of the enemy,

4. impose a judgment the enemy cannot oppose.

That is the power of decrees!

Dixon, Elizabeth (2014, February 28) Are You Decreeing and Declaring in Your Prayers? Retrieved from; https://www.charismamag.com/spirit/prayer/19877-are-you-decreeing-and-declaring-in-your-prayers. Retrieved on April 16, 2018

Dixon (2014) states the word declare comes from the Hebrew achvah, meaning "to make known" or "to set forth an accounting." It is commonly used by customs agents who ask international travelers, "Do you have anything to declare?" The agents are asking for specifics of what you have, what you are carrying.

As it pertains to us spiritually, declarations are what we speak into the atmosphere, making known what we already have possession of. We can declare our righteousness, our salvation, our eternal victory and our friendship with God.

By contrast, decrees are a tool by which we cause the truths of the heavenly realm to be manifest into the natural realm so they become our daily reality. We decree healing when we are sick. We decree provision and abundance when we are lacking. We decree peace when there is turmoil. Decrees are a tool to fulfill Matthew 6:10: "Thy Kingdom come, Thy Will be done on earth, as it is in heaven" (KJV). Decrees manifest heaven on earth. The English definition of the decree is "a statement of truth that carries the authority of a court order." For example, when a defendant is convicted of a crime and sentenced to prison, he cannot ignore that sentence because the authority of the court order is such that upon conviction, he has no further say in the matter.

The same is true with decrees in the spiritual realm. When we decree God's provision and blessings over our lives, then anything purposed against our provision and blessing can have no further say in the matter. When we decree God's peace and unity in our family, then anything purposed against peace and unity has no valid objection or standing to come against us.

The biblical context of decrees is that they are the same as the will and purposes of God. Given that serious weight in the spirit, I use only Scriptures as the basis for decrees. Often we can get our own idea of how things could or should be, but it is not uncommon for the way God unfolds His plans to look different than what we expect.

Dixon, Elizabeth (2014, February 28) Are You Decreeing and Declaring in Your Prayers? Retrieved from; https://www.charismamag.com/spirit/prayer/19877-are-you-decreeing-and-declaring-in-your-prayers. Retrieved on April 16, 2018

Now this declaring and decreeing also works for our own emotional and mental health. Declaring and decreeing has nothing to do with how you feel. All you do is take a scripture and declare it over your life. I call this call and response.

2 Timothy 1:7 (KJV)

7 For God hath not given us the spirit of fear; but of power, and of love, and of a sound mind.

So the declaration would be "According to the word of God in 2 Timothy 1:7 God has not given me a spirit of fear, therefore, I declare fear is gone in Jesus name, the love of God consumes me and I have a sound mind."

I told you about praying the scriptures. You may ask what the difference is. When you pray the scripture you are thanking God for what He has already done in the past, asking Him for what you believe He is going to do.

When you make a declaration, you are activating it in the spirit realm so it is done on earth.

Matthew 16:19 (KJV)

19 And I will give unto thee the keys of the kingdom of heaven: and whatsoever thou shalt bind on earth shall be bound in heaven: and whatsoever thou shalt loose on earth shall be loosed in heaven.

I love what the message version says,

19 "And that's not all. You will have complete and free access to God's kingdom, keys to open any and every door: no more barriers between heaven and earth, earth and heaven. A yes on earth is yes in heaven. A no on earth is no in heaven."

Matthew 18:18-19 (KJV)

18 Verily I say unto you, Whatsoever ye shall bind on earth shall be bound in heaven: and whatsoever ye shall loose on earth shall be loosed in heaven.

19 Again I say unto you, That if two of you shall agree on earth as touching any thing that they shall ask, it shall be done for them of my Father which is in heaven.

Who are the two for the sake of our text? You and the client. What do we want to bind? Fear, anxiety, depression, psychosis. You can add to the list. What do we want to release? Peace, joy, boldness, rest.

Teach the client how to declare and decree over themselves.

Lastly, Joyce Meyers said, "when the devil talks to you talk back to him." The devil talks through our thoughts, ideas, for those who experience psychosis, through audible voices. I tell my client's all the time, thoughts are like bullies you must stand up for yourself and not allow the bully to beat you up. There are examples found in the word of God. In Matthew 4 where Jesus was tempted (tested) by the devil. Jesus won the battle by declaring the word of God. He repeatedly said, "it is written" and quoted a scripture. Eventually, satan left until another opportunity came.

This is profound to me. If Jesus can talk back to the devil when He was being tested, why can't we? It didn't say Jesus ignored the devil. It didn't say He tried to drown him out with music or a grounding technique, although those things are helpful. He talked back to the devil, but he didn't say leave me alone or getaway, He used the word of God.

Let's look at the text.

Matthew 4:1-11 Living Bible (TLB)

4 Then Jesus was led out into the wilderness by the Holy Spirit, to be tempted there by Satan.

2 For forty days and forty nights he ate nothing and became very hungry.

3 Then Satan tempted him to get food by changing stones into loaves of bread.

"It will prove you are the Son of God," he said.

4 But Jesus told him, "No! For the Scriptures tell us that bread won't feed men's souls: obedience to every word of God is what we need."

5 Then Satan took him to Jerusalem to the roof of the Temple. 6 "Jump off," he said, "and prove you are the Son of God; for the Scriptures declare, 'God will send his angels to keep you from harm,' . . . they will prevent you from smashing on the rocks below."

7 Jesus retorted, "It also says not to put the Lord your God to a foolish test!"

8 Next Satan took him to the peak of a very high mountain and showed him the nations of the world and all their glory. 9 "I'll give it all to you," he said, "if you will only kneel and worship me."

10 "Get out of here, Satan," Jesus told him. "The Scriptures say, 'Worship only the Lord God. Obey only him.'"

11 Then Satan went away, and angels came and cared for Jesus.

Luke 4:13 (MSG)

13 That completed the testing. The Devil retreated temporarily, lying in wait for another opportunity.

Joyce Meyers is right sometimes it is the little things that we overlook, that have a profound effect. Jesus was our example. Again, if Jesus had to talk back to the devil what makes us think we don't have to talk back to the devil? We must talk back using scripture. We must teach our client's that it is okay to talk back to the enemy using scripture. The key is that we must use the word of God. In Luke 4 it teaches us that after Jesus was tempted, the devil only went away temporarily, the NKJV version says, "until another opportunity came." We have to teach our client's that this talking back to the enemy is not a onetime event, he will come back, thoughts will come back, to test us then we do it again. This is important because many will assume that they have failed, or digressed in a moment of weakness, but if Jesus was tempted, and the enemy came back to test him again it will happen to us.

Other ways that Jesus was tempted were through people, he had to rebuke the devil off Peter, through his disciples, through the Pharisees who were trying to test his patience because they really didn't like Him, so they kept trying to test Him. Jesus responded with the word every time. He was our example and through the word of God, we can show those we serve how to follow His example.

Our time is just about up. I hope that this book has given you a foundation of how to implement Christ and biblical strategies into mental health counseling.

It works, it really works.

It is a joy to be used by God. Nevertheless, over my years of being in the mental health field, it was disheartening to see people go through the same cycles over and over again and never come to wholeness. Healing through Christ works, but that doesn't mean everything you learned doesn't work it simply means we have to give credit back to its rightful owner Jesus. Real healing comes from Him and Him alone. Healing mental health strategies absent from Jesus is only a temporary fix and doesn't last long term.

I wish you all the blessings in the world in Christ Jesus. Before we go I have a confession. Yes, that's right I have a confession. This works. I know I am confusing you, I know I said that already. I know it works not only because it works with the client I worked with, but because it is my personal testimony. It worked for me.

My confession is.....

Well, you must read the next chapter. I wrote a book called I Am. Chapter 1 of that book was called; A Counselors Confession. I have decided to add it as a bonus chapter because I have been set free. I started with my own healing. I went through my own process. Everything I teach my client and have taught you in this book, I had to do myself. I am adding this chapter not to give you another soppy story but to encourage you as the counselor that we all go on our own journey and must come to our own place of healing. You can't bring a person to healing if you have never been there. Also, I want to encourage you through my own personal testimony that what I teach really does work. Yes, my education and background were worth it, and a great foundation. Yet, my own personal process has made me just not just another therapist but an anointed counselor.

Remember my fellow co-labors you are not average you are anointed. If anything, you read today strikes you, and you realize that you must go through your own healing do it. I still must practice what I preach. I know what my triggers are. I still must guard my heart. I realize I can't give from an empty well, so I implement strategies to refill my tank and preserve me, while I am walking through the emotional healing process for others.

My prayer and hope is that you do the same.

God Bless you

Bonus Chapter

Book: I AM

Walk in Divine Confidence, Supernatural Boldness, While Being Free From Rejection, And Emotional Wounds.

Chapter 11

A Counselor's Confession

Psalm 118:8 (KJV)

8 It is better to trust in the Lord than to put confidence in man.

I have a confession to make. As a therapist and a writer, I have spent many hears counseling, writing, and learning how to build up others. The truth is the reason why I can write this book and many others like this with such conviction is that I know my stuff. If there is one thing that I struggled with for many years, that was lack of confidence. It started as a child and grew as I grew. I never had any confidence in myself. A few months ago, I had a conference on Divine Confidence, and I told the participants my truth. I told them how I struggled with low confidence for many years. I am set free, delivered and whole now of course, but it hasn't come without a process. I didn't get confident overnight. In fact, I honestly don't remember being happy as a child. I didn't enjoy most of my twenties. I have spent more of my life self-loathing, self-defeated and insecure than I care to say. When the process of learning to love myself came, the transformation of life is,so amazing people literarily don't recognize me. I know what it is like to feel as if you are not worthy, like you're not good enough, to listen to the voice of the enemy telling you, you don't belong. I have been suicidal because I felt as though I didn't deserve to live. Oh, but God. Today I am a woman who is deeply in love with God. I love myself flaws and all. I realized confidence was not found in perfection. Confidence was not found in being the right size, the right color, the right shape, having the right degree or the right man. Confidence is found in God. Had it not been for God I don't know where I would be. My point is not to brag by any means. I have accomplished more in my life that I ever anticipated all because of God's grace, mercy, and unmerited favor. Still, none of it would have happened until I finally stopped believing the lies of the enemy and started seeing myself the way God's sees me. I write from a place of true conviction, not from the expert trying to get information to you, but as a person who has been there. I know, I understand, my misery has now become a part of my ministry. I am grateful for the finished work of Christ. Without Him, the true transformation would have never taken place. First, let's start with some interesting principles about confidence and what happens when a person is not confident.

Whenever a person is fearful on a regular basis, they lack confidence.

Whenever a person cannot effectively communicate their needs wants and desires they lack confidence.

You cannot walk in God's authority, power and presence without confidence. The anointing flows through confidence. Lack of confidence stops the move of God from flowing in your life.

What stops people from writing their book or accomplishing their goal has nothing to do with lack of resources, lack of time, but rather lack of confidence.

Ability is not confidence, but when you are confident you know your ability.

What stops people from pursuing their dreams is not lack of faith rather lack of confidence.

What stops people from speaking up even when they have something important to say that could change lives is not because they can't speak or don't know what to say rather because they lack confidence.

If when you get around someone who walks in any level of authority, and you shy away, you lack confidence.

If you become intimidated by successful people, you lack confidence.

When you are overly concerned about people's perception of you, and you worry that people won't like you, you lack self-confidence and struggle with the spirit of rejection.

When an individual never speaks up for themselves, allows other people to treat them negatively, that individual lacks confidence.

When an individual is easily offended, passive, very defensive and doesn't have a teachable spirit because they can't handle critique, these individual lacks confidence.

Lack of confidence and the spirit of rejection go hand and hand.

Lack of confidence is a barrier to your relationship with God. You can't grow in God with lack of confidence. God will tell you who He has created, you to be and you will reject His word no matter how positive and affirming they are because you lack confidence.

Low confidence is like cancer it will impacts every area of your life.

Imagine with me wanting something that is your heart's desire. You pray and pray, quote scriptures, read the Word, fast about it. Year and year, you wait for the promises of God. Maybe you are praying for a spouse; maybe you are praying for financial stability. Maybe you are praying for your ministry to take off. Year after year, you wait. Year one goes by; you wait, year two goes by you wait. Year, after year, after year, you wait. Sometimes you wait encouraged, sometimes you wait discouraged, sometimes you are content, but you know what God has promised you.

Finally, there it is, your ministry is about to take flight. You are now at the place of manifestation. Maybe you meet the spouse you have been praying for, for all those years. They are everything on your list and then some. Maybe the dream promotion is finally there; you will be the CEO of a major fortune 500 company. There you are minutes, second, days away from something you prepared for your whole life. Then something happens, and you stop dead in your tracks. You turn back around and never move forward to destiny.

What happened you may ask? Good question.

Fear happened. A little voice in your head, what we know as thoughts. The thoughts say, "you can't do that, this is too much, you're going to fail, that is not for you, you don't belong there, that person doesn't belong to you, look at them and look at you. They are perfect;

you are a mess." On and on the thoughts go. You believe your thoughts and turn around never to be seen again.

The sad truth is you can be right on the brink of the greatest breakthrough in your life and fear, lack of confidence can stop you dead in your tracks if you allow. It may sound odd for some, but it can and does happen. I can prove it. Turn with me in your Bible to Numbers 14. Before we read, let me set up the preface for you. The people of Israel had finally gotten within feet of the promise land. This is after going through hundreds of years of slavery, being released, walking through the red sea on dry land. You heard of the miracles. This is after seeing great signs wonders and miracles. Food fell from heaven, their shoes never wore out, there was a huge cloud following them to show them the way. Clearly, they had the hand of God on them. They survived great battles and won by God's hand. You would think by the time they got to the promise their confidence would be assured in God.

They get there, the place they had longed to be at and prepared for years. Regardless of the toil, struggle and stress through it all, there was one thing that they kept on their minds, they're going to the promised land.

They are right there; they can see the promise. They can't just walk up in the promise; they need to scope it out first, see what it looks like, consider if they are going to have any opposition. Moses has a bright idea;

he wants to send spies out to take a look at the land and then come back to report all that they see. This is very wise of Moses, so he does just that. This is where we will begin reading out text. We will be reading this from The Living Bible Version and the New King James Version. Let's start with Number 13.

Numbers 13:16-21 (NKJV)

16 These are the names of the men whom Moses sent to spy out the land. And Moses called Hoshea[a] the son of Nun, Joshua.

17 Then Moses sent them to spy out the land of Canaan, and said to them, "Go up this way into the South, and go up to the mountains,

18 and see what the land is like: whether the people who dwell in it are strong or weak, few or many;

19 whether the land they dwell in is good or bad; whether the cities they inhabit are like camps or strongholds;

20 whether the land is rich or poor; and whether there are forests there or not. Be of good courage. And bring some of the fruit of the land." Now the time was the season of the first ripe grapes.

21 So they went up and spied out the land from the Wilderness of Zin as far as Rehob, near the entrance of Hamath.

Numbers 13:26-33Living Bible (TLB)

26 They made their report to Moses, Aaron, and all the people of Israel in the wilderness of Paran at Kadesh, and they showed the fruit they had brought with them.

27 This was their report: "We arrived in the land you sent us to see, and it is indeed a magnificent country—a land 'flowing with milk and honey.' Here is some fruit we have brought as proof.

 28 But the people living there are powerful, and their cities are fortified and very large; and what's more, we saw Anakim giants there!

29 The Amalekites live in the south, while in the hill country there are the Hittites, Jebusites, and Amorites; down along the coast of the Mediterranean Sea and in the Jordan River Valley are the Canaanites."

30 But Caleb reassured the people as they stood before Moses. "Let us go up at once and possess it," he said, "for we are well able to conquer it!"

31 "Not against people as strong as they are!" the other spies said. "They would crush us!"

32 So the majority report of the spies was negative: "The land is full of warriors, the people are powerfully built,

33 and we saw some of the Anakim there, descendants of the ancient race of giants. We felt like grasshoppers before them, they were so tall!"

Are you seeing what happened here? In the King James Version, it reads,

Numbers 13:33 King James Version (KJV)

33 And there we saw the giants, the sons of Anak, which come of the giants: and we were in our own sight as grasshoppers, and so we were in their sight

Notice all they did was a spy out the land. They didn't have an argument with the Anakim people. There was no indication that the Anakim people even saw them. The Anakim people didn't say they were grasshoppers, the people of Israel assumed that the Anakim people saw them as grasshoppers.

My point is what was really stopping them from going into the promise was not the enemy, it was their perception of how them saw themselves. Maybe they were weaker than the enemy. Maybe the enemy could defeat them. Still, they had God on their side and promise from God. This is why confidence is not found in our ability, it is found in God. When they cried out, they were saying, "we can't do this." They also were doubting that God would get them the promise land. They lacked trust in God. When a Christians have low or no confidence they really don't trust God.

Now let's go to Number 14. We have to look at how low confidence spreads. We also have to consider God's response. As a warning, it was not pretty. God was not empathic towards their wrong perception, in fact, He took great offense to them. He decided that all those who doubted who were not fit to get to the promise. Come with met let's read the text together.

Numbers 14:1-11Living Bible (TLB)

14 Then all the people began weeping aloud, and they carried on all night.

2 Their voices rose in a great chorus of complaint against Moses and Aaron.

"We wish we had died in Egypt," they wailed, "or even here in the wilderness,

3 rather than be taken into this country ahead of us. Jehovah will kill us there, and our wives and little ones will become slaves. Let's get out of here and return to Egypt!"

4 The idea swept the camp. "Let's elect a leader to take us back to Egypt!" they shouted.

5 Then Moses and Aaron fell face downward on the ground before the people of Israel.

6 Two of the spies, Joshua (the son of Nun), and Caleb (the son of Jephunneh), ripped their clothing

7 and said to all the people, "It is a wonderful country ahead,

8 and the Lord loves us. He will bring us safely into the land and give it to us. It is very fertile, a land 'flowing with milk and honey'!

9 Oh, do not rebel against the Lord, and do not fear the people of the land. For they are but bread for us to eat! The Lord is with us and he has removed his protection from them! Don't be afraid of them!"

10-11 But the only response of the people was to talk of stoning them. Then the glory of the Lord appeared, and the Lord said to Moses, "How long will these people despise me? Will they never believe me, even after all the miracles I have done among them?

After the spies came back, they gave a bad report. Nevertheless, Joshua and Caleb were different, they were confident that God who brought them through the wilderness would indeed get them to the promise.

Cleary the people of Israel were not interested in hearing what they had to say. Look at God's response.

Numbers 14:26-30Living Bible (TLB)

26-27 Then the Lord said to Moses and to Aaron, "How long will this wicked nation complain about me? For I have heard all that they have been saying.

28 Tell them, 'The Lord vows to do to you what you feared:

29 You will all die here in this wilderness! Not a single one of you twenty years old and older, who has complained against me,

30 shall enter the Promised Land. Only Caleb (son of Jephunneh) and Joshua (son of Nun) are permitted to enter it.

What is your promise? What have you been praying to God about? What would your response be if when you finally see it, it is so vast, so huge, that it intimidates you? My point is you can be right at the brink of the greatest breakthrough of your life and lack of confidence in God can stop you dead in your tracks, and stop you from entering the thing your heart has spent years preparing, praying, struggling and fighting for. By the way the people of Israel who didn't respond well didn't make to the thing that God had promised them.

Numbers 14:37-38Living Bible (TLB)

36-38 Then the ten spies who had incited the rebellion against Jehovah by striking fear into the hearts of the people were struck dead before the Lord. Of all the spies, only Joshua and Caleb remained alive.

Just because you have a promise from God that doesn't mean you will make it to the promise. A delay is not always a delay; sometimes it is a denial. God is not going to force His promises on you; if you don't want what He has for you, He will respect your wishes.

What say you? Can you determine in your mind, to make it to the promise?

As a therapist we must walk in divine confidence. When we teach the client's we serve the principles of CCBT they will walk in divine confidence.

THE POWER IS FOUND IN THE I AM
I AM
I AM
WALK IN DIVINE CONFIDENCE, SUPERNATURAL
BOLDNESS, WHILE BEING FREE FROM
REJECTION, AND EMOTIONAL WOUNDS
SAMARIA M COLBERT
SAMARIA M COLBERT

Burns, David D., MD. 1989. The Feeling Good Handbook. New York: William Morrow and Company)

Crabtree, Candace (n.d) Praying The Scripture, Retrieved from; https://mercyisnew.com/praying-scriptures, Retrieved on April 10, 2018.

Cognitive Restructuring: Socratic Questions (Worksheet) (n.d) | Therapist Aid https://www.therapistaid.com/therapy-worksheet/socratic-questioning. Retrieved April 10, 2018.

Common Interventions Terminology and Documentation (n.d) Retrieved from; https://www.pinterest.com/pin/374502525234570323/?autologin =true April 3, 2018.

Codependent Relationships (n.d) http://www.webmd.com/sex-relationships/features/signs-of-a-codependent-relationship#1. Retrieved on March 20, 2017

Copeland, Kenneth (n.d) 5 Benefits of Speaking In Tongues Retrieved from; http://www.kcm.org/real-help/prayer/apply/5-benefits-praying-tongues. Retrieved on April 16, 2018.

Counseling Intake Form (n.d) https://www.pinterest.com/pin/733383120540157290 Retrieved on October 30, 2017

Counseling Plan Template (n.d) As found at http://thebridgesummit.co/counseling-treatment-plan-templateretrieved on October 30, 2017

Covert Incest (n.d) Retrieved from https://en.wikipedia.org/wiki/Covert_incest. Retrieved on April 20, 2017

Cycle of Poverty (n.d)
https://en.wikipedia.org/wiki/Cycle_of_poverty. Retrieved on
March 17, 2018.

Defense Mechanism.
https://en.wikipedia.org/wiki/Defence_mechanisms. Retrieved
on March 30, 2017.

Defense Mechanisms. (n.d)
https://www.merriamwebster.com/dictionary/defense%20mecha
nism. Retrieved March 20, 2017

Dixon, Elizabeth (2014, February 28) Are You Decreeing and
Declaring in Your Prayers? Retrieved from;
https://www.charismamag.com/spirit/prayer/19877-are-you-
decreeing-and-declaring-in-your-prayers. Retrieved on April 16,
2018

Dixon, Elizabeth (2014, February 28) Are You Decreeing and
Declaring in Your Prayers? Retrieved from;
https://www.charismamag.com/spirit/prayer/19877-are-you-
decreeing-and-declaring-in-your-prayers. Retrieved on April 16,
2018

Do You Have 'Victim Mentality'? What To Do About It (2010,
Dec 18) https://www.huffingtonpost.com/morty-lefkoe/victim-
mentality_b_794628.html Retrieved April 15, 2018

Emotional Affair (n.d) Retrieved from,
https://en.wikipedia.org/wiki/Emotional_affair. Retrieved on
March 20, 2017

Emotional Covert Incest When Parents Make Their Kids, Their
Partner (n.d) https://www.goodtherapy.org/blog/emotional-
covert-incest-when-parents-make-their-kids-partners-0914165.
Retrieved on March 20, 2017

Forgiveness (n.d). Retrieved from Greater Good Magazine. https://greatergood.berkeley.edu/topic/forgiveness/definition. Retrieved on April 1, 2018

How Israel Complaining 14 times mirrors your Christian Journey. (n.d) Retrieved from. https://onelordonebody.com/2014/02/27/how-israel-complaining-14-times-mirrors-your-christian-journey/. Retrieved on April 16, 2018.

Intake Assessment (n.d) Retrieved from; https://www.pinterest.com/pin/118008452712221724/ October 30, 2017.

Imposter Syndrome (n.d) https://en.wikipedia.org/wiki/Impostor_syndrome. Retrieved April 15, 2018,

Learned Helplessness (n.d) https://en.wikipedia.org/wiki/Learned_helplessness. Retrieved on April 15, 2018

Masking Personality (n.d) https://en.wikipedia.org/wiki/Masking_(personality)Retrieved on March 20, 2017

Maslow Hiearchy of Needs (n.d) Retrieved from. https://www.google.com/imgres?imgurl=https://www.simplypsychology.org/maslow.jpg&imgrefurl. Retrieved on March 20, 2017

Mcleod. S (2015). Cognitive Behavioral Therapy. Retrieved from https://www.simplypsychology.org/cognitive-therapy.html Retrieved on April 1, 2018

Mcleod. S (2015). Cognitive Behavioral Therapy. Retrieved from https://www.simplypsychology.org/cognitive-therapy.html Retrieved on April 1, 2018

Mental Health Intake (n.d) Retrieved from;
https://www.pinterest.com/explore/mental-health-assessment/
(n.d) October 30, 2017.

Mental Health Status (n.d.) Retrieved from:
https://www.pinterest.com/pin/405957353883101655 October
30, 2017.

Parentification (n.d)
https://en.wikipedia.org/wiki/Parentification. Retrieved on
March 20, 2017.

Progress Notes Client (n.d) As found;
http://www.notebuilder.com/NoteTOC/ProgressNotes.htm
Retrieved on April 3, 2018

Rosenbluth, T (2013, October 15). Where do our thoughts
originate? Retrieved from
https://www.israelnationalnews.com/Blogs/Message.aspx/5343
on February 28, 2018

Rosilind, Jukic. (2016, July 18) 6 Reasons This Popular
Meditation Trend Is Dangerous for Christians. Retrieved from,
https://www.charismanews.com/opinion/58612-6-reasons-this-
popular-meditation-trend-is-dangerous-for-christians on April
16, 2018.

Safe in His Arms lyrics © Warner/Chappell Music, Inc

4 Symptoms of the Orphan Spirit in Church Life. (2012
September 17).
https://www.enlivenpublishing.com/blog/2012/09/17/4-
symptoms-of-the-orphan-spirit-in-church-life/ Retrieved on
April 15, 2018

Thought Stopping (n.d)
https://en.wikipedia.org/wiki/Thoght_stopping. Retrieved on
March 26, 2018.

Two Wolves (n.d) http://www.virtuesforlife.com/two-wolves/ Retrieved on March 28, 2018.

Treatment Plan (n.d) As found at; https://www.goodtherapy.org/blog/psychpedia/treatment-plan October 30, 2017.

Treatment Plan Review (n.d) As found at; https://www.pinterest.com/janejackson513/goals-objectives-interventions/ Retrieved on October 30, 2017

Socrative Questions (n.d) https://www.therapistaid.com/worksheets/socratic-questioning.pdf. Retrieved April 10, 2018.

Smart Goals Worksheet (n.d) As found at; https://www.pinterest.com/pin/560698222329176340, Retrieved on October 30, 2017.

Valloton, Kris (n.d) 7 Signs Of Unhealthy Soul Ties. Retrieved from http://krisvallotton.com/7-signs-of-an-unhealthy-soul-tie/. Retrieved on March 20, 2017.

About The Author:

Samaria was saved at eight years old. Shortly after that she received the baptism of the Holy Ghost. Samaria first received her call to ministry many years ago when attended to Bennett College in Greensboro, NC. After attending a youth-led Bible study, she learned that some things only come through fasting and prayer. The Lord impressed upon her to seek His face for what she needed to hear from Him. It was then that Samaria began to seek God for her purpose and destiny within the body of Christ. So after much prayer and fasting, God spoke to Samaria in a series of dreams and visions over a three year period. It was during this time that she experienced some of the greatest spiritual awakenings of her life. Her confidence in her relationship with God and His destiny for her life was certain.

Samaria Colbert is an anointed writer, licensed therapist, minister and consultant. She received her Bachelor's degree from Bowie State University, in Bowie, MD. She later went on to receive her Master's from Howard University, in Washington, D.C. She is currently pursuing a Ph.D. Samaria calls North Carolina home.

Samaria also has a heart to counsel; she is the founder and CEO of Kingdom Creative Counseling Services. The counseling part of her private practice is specifically for women, men, and children who have survived early childhood sexual abuse and domestic violence. Samaria uses an integrative approach to therapy that includes, mental health, inner healing, and deliverance, all biblically based so that complete healing and wholeness is achieved through Christ Jesus.

Samaria is also the founder and CEO of LIKEAPRO Professional Writing Services. An organization dedicated to a spirit of excellence and completing the writing projects for Christian professionals, lay persons, and fivefold ministers.

Samaria uses her skills and passion as a writer, teacher to develop informational training materials and conduct workshops on how to effectively use integrative therapy techniques in counseling practice.

She believes in, "Absolute abandonment for the cost of the call of Jesus Christ." Samaria is a young woman, who loves God, loves His word, and is passionate above all about His purpose and destiny for her life.

Stay tuned, the future looks bright, and there is so much more to come from this dynamic, anointed and appointed a woman of God.

"What will you do in your lifetime that will have an impact on someone else's life for a lifetime?"

Samaria M. Colbert

To stay up to date with her latest writing projects, ministry and to request her to speak at your event please visit her website.

www.samariacolbert.com

www.likeaprowritingservices.com

www.kingdomcreativecounseling.com

Insurance accepted

336-543-0159

www.kingdomcreativecounseling.com

Depression   Christ-Centered

Anxiety   Psychotic Disorders

Recovery from Early Child Sexual Abuse/Trauma

Domestic Violence   Recovery from Spiritual Abuse
Inner Healing and Deliverance

Play Therapy

Adults, Families, and Children Served

www.samariacolbert.com

www.likeaprowritingservices.com

LikeAPro Professional Writing Services

Make sure you pick up your very own copy of Samaria's other books:

No Promise Without A Process The Makings Of A True Prophet

The Wisdom To Fulfilling Your Prophetic Destiny. A Memoir of Words, Warnings, And Pitfalls To Avoid Missing Your Prophetic Destiny.

This I know: Because There Are Choices You Make That Can Either Birth or Abort Your Spiritual Destiny

God Can Change Anyone

No Promise Without A Process The Makings Of A True Prophet Part II

Inside Out Because Real Transformations Happens From The Inside Out Not The Outside In

To Whom It May Concern

Wisdom, Warnings and Warfare

Hearing The Voice of God

Demons, Deliverance and Spiritual Warfare

Soul Ties

Not Without A Struggle

Trusting God Is Not Easy But It Is Worth It

Not Without A Purpose

Deliverance From Depression

No More Fear

You Are Not Forgotten

The Process of Emotional Healing

The Process of Emotional Healing Workbook

The Process of Emotional Healing Facilitators Guide

A Ready Made Writer

Hidden To Lead

Healing The Heart Through Forgiveness

The Ministry of Honor

Broken

Kingdom Mandates, Kingdom Mantles and Kingdom Authority

The Heart Of Worship

Restoration

Psychological Warfare

The Wait

The Wait Individual Workbook

The Wait Facilitators Guide

The Wait 60 Day Devotional

Christian Cognitive Behavioral Therapy

Let Down Your Nets

The Bible And Business

Who Beguiled You?

According To Your Faith

Couches and Conversations Workbook Journal

Couches and Conversations Group Manual

Couches and Conversations book

I Am

Fight Fear With Faith Workbook

A Workbook for Individuals and Groups

CHRISTIAN COGNITIVE BEHAVIORAL THERAPY

SAMARIA M COLBERT

SAMARIA M. COLBERT
PSYCHOLOGICAL
WARFARE
HOW SATAN USES THE MOST VIAL, DIABOLICAL,
AND DANGEROUS WEAPON KNOWN TO MANKIND

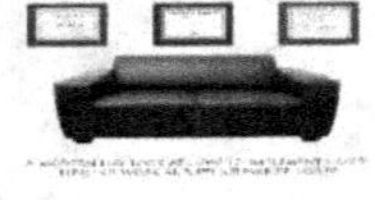

Couches and Conversations
TRAININGS COMING IN 2018

God the Father wants His children healed, whole, set free and delivered from all emotional wounds. Inner healing is a counseling ministry that God has ordained for Christian counselors, therapists, and ministers. Inner Healing is NOT the same as traditional mental health counseling. The author has a mandate from heaven to train Christian leaders to do the work of counseling ministry. This series includes the book;

- Couches and Conversations (Teaches Basic Inner Healing principles)
- Couches and Conversations (Journal Workbook)
- Couches and Conversations (For small group)
- Couches and Conversations (Teaches Inner Healing Implementation, and Methodology)

Coming in 2018 Training and Seminars for (Christian Therapist, Clinicians and Counseling Ministers).

CONTACT US IF YOU ARE INTERESTED IN SCHEDULING A TRAINING AND PRICING. VISIT THE CONTACT TAB

BOOKS AND TRAINING MATERIAL AVAILABLE DEC 1, 2017 VISIT THE BOOKSTORE TO PURCHASE, ALSO AVAILABLE ON AMAZON AND KINDLE

Kingdom Institute For Training Christian Professionals

K.I.T.C.P

For more information contact us by visiting the website
at:

www.samariacolbert.com

www.samariacolbert.com

281

www.samariacolbert.com

www.likeaprowritingservices.com

www.kingdomcreativecounseling.com

www.samariacolbert.com

www.likeaprowritingservices.com

www.kingdomcreativecounseling.com

www.ingramcontent.com/pod-product-compliance
Lightning Source LLC
Chambersburg PA
CBHW070109260726
48658CB00001B/45